D0712286

Top-Down Vision
and
Bottom-Up Management

Other Books by Larry Goddard

Corporate Intensive Care
Why Businesses Fail and How to Make Them Succeed
(York, 1993)

The Turbocharged Company
Igniting Your Business to Soar Ahead of the Competition
(York, 1995)

Top-Down Vision
and
Bottom-Up Management

A Collaborative
and Motivational
Path to
Business Success

Larry Goddard
and
the Parkland Team

Printed in the United States of America
06 05 04 03 10 9 8 7 6 5 4 3 2 1

Edited by Brenda L. Lewison
Jacket and Text Design by Sheila Hart Design, Inc.

For volume purchases and discounts, contact York Publishing at 216/491-0231 (phone), 216/491-0251 (fax).

Publisher's Cataloging in Publication
Goddard, Larry.
    Top-down vision and bottom-up management: a collaborative and
motivational path to business success / Larry Goddard and the Parkland Team. – 1st ed.
    p. cm.
    Includes index.
    LCCN 2002103574
    ISBN 0-9634940-9-0 (cloth)

    1. Strategic planning.
    2. Strategic planning— Employee participation.
    3. Business planning.
    4. Industrial management—Employee participation. I. Title.

HD30.28.G53 2002   658.4'012
                              QB102-200484

The Parkland Team
Co-authors, advisors and editors

Jenny Alexander
Domenic Aversa
David Cesar
Rita Dawson
Dr. Ronald Fountain
Mark Frater
Tira Hawkins
Phillip Jones
Dan Kiehl
Mark Kozel
Christina Lucas
Randy Markey
Miles Molyneaux
Michael Nuremberg
David Sanders
Wayne Vespoli
Amy Whitacre

To the thousands of people who
have tirelessly and enthusiastically
participated in Top-Down Vision
and Bottom-Up Management
implementations at so many of
our valued client companies

Contents

Exhibits xii
Foreword xv
Preface xix

Part I: Top-Down Vision 1
A New Partnership 3
The Ultimate Responsibility 7
Painting a Picture 9
Surviving, Thriving or Diving 11
The "Aha!" Test 15
Leading to Success 17
20/20 Vision 21
The True VIPs 25
Buy-in 27
Overview of the Process 31
Context 35
Vision 45
Components of the Vision Statement 53
Vision Filters 61
Follow the Leader 67
Verify the Vision 69

Part II: Bottom-Up Management 73
Tilt the Playing Field 75

Two Heads Are Better Than One 77

Types of Teams. 83

Strategies 87

Drivers of Success. 93

Strategy Components 97

Tactics 99

Tactics Components 107

Part III: Bottom-Up Management Tools **109**

Tool 1-Lean 111

  Lean, But Not Mean 113

  Becoming Lean 119

  Lean Principles 121

  Setting Up for Success 127

  Error Proofing 133

  Going with the Flow 137

  Takt Time. 145

  Benefits of Lean 149

Tool 2- Kaizen 151

  Good Change 153

  The Kaizen Process 155

Tool 3- Real Accounting 159

  RAAP with GAAP 161

  Real-Time Information 163

  Activity-Based Costing: ABC 165

  Making the Right Decisions with ABC. 171

  Accountability 175

  Performance Data 177

Tool 4 – Brainstorming and Analytical Techniques 179

    Brainstorming 181

    Fishbone Diagrams 185

    Storyboarding 187

    Consensus Building 193

    Mind Mapping 197

    The Change Loop 201

    Pareto Analysis 203

    Facilitation Techniques and Skills 205

Tool 5- Gainsharing 209

    Laser Focus 211

    Incentive Compensation Plan Considerations 213

Part IV: Conclusion **217**

Plan to Succeed 219

Appendixes:

    1. Checklist for Current State Analysis 223

    2. Set-up Observation Form 227

    3. Process Documentation Form 229

    4. Sample Daily Flash Report 231

    5. Sample Hourly Tracking Chart 233

Glossary 235

Index 243

Exhibits

Part I: Top-Down Vision

1.1   The Collaboration Zone 2

1.2   Allocation of a Leader's Energies
         in a TDVBUM Environment 6

1.3   Information: Essential Ingredient 22

1.4   The Buy-in Process 26

1.5   Top-Down Vision and Bottom-Up
         Management Process 30

1.6   Top-Down Vision and Bottom-Up
         Management Process (Context) 34

1.7   Examples of Strengths & Weaknesses,
         Opportunities & Threats 37

1.8   Opportunities & Threats Prioritized 38

1.9   Market Structure Analysis:
         Porter's Five Forces 40

1.10   Industry Evolution Analysis 43

1.11   Top-Down Vision and Bottom-Up
         Management Process (Vision) 44

1.12   Future Market Leader Profile Example
         & Gap Analysis 49

1.13   Vision Statement Components Template
         (Vision Elements) 52

1.14   Vision Statement 55

1.15   Top-Down Vision and Bottom-Up
         Management Process (Vision Filters) 60

Part II: Bottom-Up Management

2.1   Traditional Business Process
        and Information Flow 78

2.2   Team-Based Horizontal Organization 79

2.3   Top-Down Vision and Bottom-Up
        Management Process (Strategies) 86

2.4   Strategy Gap 88

2.5   Strategy Development 89

2.6   Using the 80:20 Rule to Guide Strategies
        to Maximize Vision 90

2.7   Drivers of Success 95

2.8   Vision Statement Components Template
        (Strategy Components) 96

2.9   Top-Down Vision and Bottom-Up Management
        Process (Tactics) 98

2.10   Vision Statement Action Plan 101

2.11   Action Plan Details 102

2.12   Vision, Strategies & Tactics 105

2.13   Vision Statement Components Template
        (Tactics Components) 106

Part III: Bottom-Up Management Tools

3.1.1   Seven Buckets of Waste: Non-Value-Added
        Activities 118

3.1.2   Typical Batch Manufacturing Chart 123

3.1.3   Typical Continuous Flow or Cellular
        Manufacturing Layout 124

3.1.4   Comparison of Lean Conversion 125

3.1.5   Stage 1: Intermingled Setup Reduction 128

3.1.6   Stage 2: Separated-Stage Setup Reduction . . . 129

3.1.7   Stage 3: Converted Work Setup Reduction . . 130

3.1.8   Stage 4: Advanced-Stage Setup Reduction. . . 131

3.1.9   Value Stream Mapping (Current State Map) . 139

3.1.10 Value Stream Mapping (Future State Map). . 140

3.1.11 Takt Time Calculation 144

3.1.12 The Ideal Loading 147

3.2.1   Common Non-Value-Added Activities 156

3.3.1   Using Variable Costing and Activity-Based
        Costing to Make Operating Decisions 170

3.3.2   Using Full-Absorption Accounting to
        Make Operating Decisions. 173

3.4.1   Fishbone Diagram 184

3.4.2   Listing Possible Causes of a Problem 188

3.4.3   Categorizing Causes of a Problem 189

3.4.4   Prioritizing Causes of a Problem 190

3.4.5   Mind Mapping 196

3.4.6   The Change Loop 200

3.4.7   Pareto Analysis 202

Foreword

Top-Down Vision and Bottom-Up Management (TDVBUM) is both a book and a philosophy on how to take charge of a company, marshaling all of its resources to achieve performance goals and objectives through teamwork. I recommend both the book and the philosophy to anyone who is serious about competing and succeeding in today's world of rapid-fire change.

I was first introduced to the principles of TDVBUM a little more than one year ago. My family's 90-year-old, third-generation ceramic tile manufacturing and distribution business was thrust into a "down" business cycle that was exacerbated by record-high levels of low-priced imported tile and a debt structure that was stifling the company. These factors contributed to the closure and liquidation of one of our three tile manufacturing facilities, the consolidation of our two other tile manufacturing facilities, and to the "right-sizing" of all of the rest of our operations, from top to bottom.

With the help of Larry Goddard and the professionals at The Parkland Group, we first set out to assess the challenges and opportunities that faced our company, internally and externally. We soon had a pretty clear picture of the scope and magnitude of it all. Even though the case for reform was compelling, we had great trepidation. My brothers and I knew that we were embarking on a path that would not be business-as-usual. It was not a comfortable experience to question so many of the practices, beliefs and people (including ourselves) that we had taken for granted for many years. Many soul-searching and emotional meetings were held before all members of our family and management were ready to buy in to the changes that were needed.

In too many corners of the company, the approach to daily tasks had more to do with "this is the way we have always done it" than it did to the sort of clearly defined action plans and performance standards that are the mark of first-rate corporations. The policies that we did have in place seemed more grounded in our own internal paths of least resistance than in what was being demanded by the customers. Our business was sick and needed intensive care.

Armed with a strategic assessment that was, frankly, staggering in its proportions, we started by putting together a Vision and strategic plan centered on team-based activity. New goals and objectives for a whole range of company functions were established, along with appropriate performance standards and time frames. A new accountability was to be demanded of everyone. This was the Top-Down Vision component of our program. And it set the stage for sweeping changes to come.

Flowing from this Vision, cross-functional teams, nominated by fellow employees and not by management, were put together throughout the company. They developed tactical plans with specific, detailed action points for every division of the company. They then set out to separate the non-value added activities from the value-added activities of virtually every department. It was the task of these employee teams to take the Vision and apply the principles of Bottom-Up Management. Where more intensive teamwork was required, three-day Kaizens were facilitated by professionals from The Parkland Group. Soon, the positive effects of Bottom-Up Management were becoming evident to senior management and rank-and-file alike.

After several months of TDVBUM, goals that were thought to be impossible started to look realistic. Defeatist attitudes that had been in the way of achieving even small successes were replaced by a can-do approach. Successes built on one another bit by bit, leading to bigger successes. Results started to be reflected in our performance.

Would I have believed, for instance, that we could liquidate five million square feet of closeout products in a time frame and at a price point that beat our projections with our bank? No, but we did. Or, would anyone have thought it was possible to wrench out multiple twenty percent and thirty percent productivity improvements within individual departments in our factories? No, but we did! And we did much more, including introducing a new outsourcing program that will be a critical part of our future.

One of the hardest changes for me personally was the shift from a hands-on manager to a coach and cheerleader. As time went by I became more comfortable trusting Bottom-Up Management—and I really enjoyed seeing people grow and thrive on the new responsibility. I could literally see their buy-in growing on a daily basis.

I was particularly pleased and, to be frank, surprised by how well our employees responded to and dealt with the challenges presented to them as part of this process. Many were asked to work extra hours participating on teams or implementing changes. Several were asked to commute as we moved production to a sister plant and, regrettably, many were required to leave our organization as a result of cost-cutting, plant closures and efficiency improvements. Throughout this process, morale remained positive, with the vast majority of people willing to chip in wherever needed.

As of this writing, we have new and even more far-reaching performance goals and objectives underway that will result in operating improvements in the millions of dollars. TDVBUM will be central to achieving these results and, ultimately, to regenerating our company, shaping it back into the profitable, growing enterprise that it had been for so many years. There will be setbacks all along the journey that will require additional difficult decisions. And there will be disappointments— lots of them. But the beauty of Top-Down Vision and Bottom-Up Management is that it is an interpretive, evolving, and self-correcting kind of management philosophy.

As a CEO, one of the greatest benefits was learning how to share the load. There were days in the past when it seemed like I had the weight of the entire company on my shoulders. Now the load is shared by many others. The challenges are still there, but they are more manageable. Top-Down Vision and Bottom-Up Management has made a great difference in my life and business.

Larry Goddard and his capable team at The Parkland Group have now put their TDVBUM down on paper in this concise, yet thorough, book. I recommend it to any serious management team that is facing the kinds of external and internal challenges that my company has faced. I encourage you to learn all that you can from it, trusting it will take you to places you may otherwise have only dreamed about.

David W. Johnson
CEO, Summitville Tiles, Inc.
Summitville, Ohio

Preface

Observing a successful, well-run business is an extremely rewarding experience. People are energized and motivated, activities are efficient and productive, customers are appreciative, and financial stakeholders are happy. Achieving this state is not overwhelmingly difficult. It can be a very realistic and attainable goal for most businesses. Regretfully, only a very small percentage of businesses capitalize on the opportunities available to help them reach that successful state.

Less than twenty percent of the energy used by a typical incandescent light bulb is utilized to create light. The vast majority of the energy generates heat, an output of little, if any, value. A similar phenomenon happens in businesses. Energy is wasted on activities that are not focused on a specific target that will lead the company to success.

Top-Down Vision and Bottom-Up Management is a process that allows organizations of all types and sizes to focus on actions that will lead to success. It is based on the belief that employees want to be part of a success story and they will share their energy and talents generously. When employees are given this chance, most companies experience remarkable gains in creativity, productivity and morale.

Prior to establishing The Parkland Group in 1989, I became the chief executive officer of Waco International Corporation at the age of twenty-nine. A manufacturer and distributor of construction products and supplies, Waco had been quite successful in the past, but had fallen into significant disrepair and was losing large amounts of money.

As I set out to develop a turnaround plan, I did extensive research on the literature for leaders in similar positions. I was particularly interested in developing a Vision for the company and learning what the components and makeup of that Vision should be. I never found anything that met my needs. Consequently, I began to develop my own approach, a very rough version of the Top-Down Vision and Bottom-Up Management process described in this book. This approach served Waco well, facilitating a more than tenfold increase in revenues, healthy profits and a public stock exchange listing.

The process has evolved over the years and has become significantly more defined in the last five years. Many of my colleagues at Parkland have made major contributions to the process during this time. In fact, we use Top-Down Vision and Bottom-Up Management to run our own consulting business and we have introduced it to most of our clients over the past ten years. It has been the foundation of exceptional success for our clients and for us.

Top-Down Vision and Bottom-Up Management starts with the development of the Vision for a business, taking into account all aspects of the current environment, or context, in which the business operates. It describes to the entire organization where they are heading and, just as important, why that path is likely to lead to success. The Vision must paint a picture of what the future will look like and motivate the entire organization. It must provide enough information to help people make decisions that are consistent with it. Employees need and deserve this clear direction. Without it, their efforts will be inefficient, lacking focus and unity.

Corporate Visions must be much more than missions, generalized goals or "feel-good" statements. The guidance they give to the organization needs to be comprehensive and specific. Through our research, we have developed a list of the elements and components that are essential for a Vision statement. Because the Vision is so important to the success of the organization, its development and communication are the domain of senior management. While it is important to obtain feedback from people throughout the company, this is one responsibility that cannot be delegated.

But Top-Down Vision is only the start of the process. The energy, creativity and success are achieved from the involvement of employees throughout the company in figuring out how to turn the dream into reality. Going far beyond empowerment, Bottom-Up Management is a true partnership between management and employees, who all commit to a Vision and utilize their collective talents to achieve it through a collaborative and mutually respectful process. The Bottom-Up Management process we have developed provides a comprehensive, yet flexible, approach for employees at all levels to follow. With the guidance and direction of a clear and well-communicated Vision, it can be a phenomenally successful and enjoyable path to execution of a plan for business success.

Most employees adapt very easily, but they do need training in the concepts of Top-Down Vision and Bottom-Up Management. To facilitate this, we have developed five Bottom-Up Management tools that give managers and employees new skills and approaches for channeling their creativity and improving their effectiveness, both as individuals and as team members.

When I set out to write this book, it immediately became obvious that it must be done in a Top-Down Vision and Bottom-Up Management manner because the process is so central to our firm. I developed a Vision for the book and wrote an outline and the first 10,000 words. Then we held a firm-wide meeting where I presented the Vision and outline and asked volunteers to help complete the book. Everyone offered to help with various aspects, including planning, writing, researching, design and editing. Many meetings were held to discuss approaches and content. As the book developed, drafts were circulated to all team members for review, suggestions, comments and editing. Any disagreements we encountered were worked out through brainstorming.

It was very gratifying to include all members of the Parkland team in this definition of a methodology that can help businesses across the globe. I am indebted to everyone for the personal time they sacrificed for this project. Their outstanding contributions made this book a vastly better one than I could have created alone, a testament to the value of Top-Down Vision and Bottom-Up Management. The result is a book that is a source of great pride and satisfaction to all of us.

My colleagues and I are also deeply indebted to our editor, Brenda Lewison, who did a superb job in bringing clarity and focus to our words; to our publisher, Rachal Rapoport from York Publishing, whose advice and guidance were invaluable; and to our designer, Sheila Hart, who gave the book its clear and elegant presentation. A million thanks to all the friends, family, clients and business colleagues who read the manuscripts, examined dust jacket and interior designs and provided such valuable feedback and advice. All of you contributed significantly to making this a better book.

Learning is a continuous process. We at Parkland are dedicated to the never-ending process of finding new ways to help improve the performance and values of our clients' businesses. We would be delighted to hear from readers in order to learn from their experiences as we continue to enhance the Top-Down Vision and Bottom-Up Management method.

Larry Goddard
Cleveland, Ohio
tpg@parkland.com

Part I

Top-Down Vision

"Would you tell me, please, which way I ought to walk from here?"

"That depends a good deal on where you want to get to," said the Cat.

"I don't much care where," said Alice.

"Then it doesn't matter which way you walk," said the Cat.

"Alice's Adventures in Wonderland"
Lewis Carroll

Exhibit 1.1

The Collaboration Zone

Top-Down Vision

Collaboration Zone

Bottom-Up Management

A New Partnership
Command-and-control management is dead

The business world has never been more competitive, changing at breakneck speed. Many conditions that were typical or predictable a short while ago are obsolete or erratic today. Witness the dot-com phenomenon which catapulted from obscurity to a financial earthquake; many of these businesses plummeted from adulation to ridicule in less than five years. Despite these challenging conditions, some companies thrive in this environment, growing while their competitors collapse. We believe we know why.

Over the past ten years, while working with more than 200 under-performing businesses, the consultants at The Parkland Group have been studying why some businesses excel and others fail. Many of our conclusions were documented in *Corporate Intensive Care*[1] and *The Turbocharged Company*.[2]

Business success is very closely tied to how well management and employees collaborate.

Since publication of these books, the successes we witnessed at so many of our clients have increased our optimism about opportunities for dramatic business improvement. For those willing to embrace new ideas and practices, success can be an attainable goal, even under the toughest conditions.

We found that success is very closely correlated to how well

---

1. Larry Goddard, *Corporate Intensive Care*, York, 1993.
2. Larry Goddard and David Brown, *The Turbocharged Company*, York, 1995.

management and employees at all levels work together. To achieve consistent and lasting success, traditional relationships must change. Instead of command-and-control strategies, so prevalent in the past, a new interdependent business structure is essential. Companies must achieve a unique alliance between management and employees, in which they share common goals and responsibility for achieving them.

This structure functions as a collaborative partnership, with each party playing different, yet vitally important, roles. Senior management is responsible for developing and communicating an inspirational direction for the business, indicating where it is heading, or its "Vision." This Vision is then shared with employees throughout the company ("Top-Down Vision").

Top-Down Vision and Bottom-Up Management works equally well for companies of all sizes and circumstances.

With clarity about the broad goals and motivated by the Vision, employees at all levels become involved in determining how to make the Vision a reality ("Bottom-Up Management"). This new partnership, created by giving employees the responsibility and tools to participate in implementing the Vision, can produce outstanding results.

Until the last decade of the twentieth century, military-style command-and-control management was predominant in the business world. Managers did the thinking and told employees what to do; workers were not encouraged to think. The extreme competitive forces of the current environment do not allow businesses to survive with this approach. They need the creativity and energy that are generated from collaboration. They also need the clarity of direction generated from Top-Down Vision and Bottom-Up Management ("TDVBUM"). The improvements in communications resulting from the

Internet, e-mail and voice mail facilitate the more open and less hierarchical organizations that are essential to TDVBUM.

Top-Down Vision and Bottom-Up Management works equally well for companies of all sizes and circumstances. It is just as relevant to the corner grocery store as it is to a Fortune 500 company.[3] It works for growth companies, mature businesses and turnaround situations. The starting point is developing a Vision for the business that will lead it to success. This Vision becomes the guiding light, establishing the rationale and inspiration for all future decisions.

Developing a company's business plan or strategy has always been the responsibility of senior management. The management style that dominated the business world until recently, however, usually did not emphasize communicating the plan to employees throughout the business or involving them in seeking solutions. That structure deprived many businesses of invaluable creativity and energy that was available to build and sustain their competitive advantages and profitability.

This book sets out a practical and stimulating path for change through an interdependent alliance of management and employees. Top-Down Vision and Bottom-Up Management offers all businesses[4] an enormous benefit: the ability to capitalize on opportunities and the extensive in-house talent waiting to be unleashed.

---

3. Because larger companies are usually more complex, having multiple business units, the application of the TDVBUM process must be adapted to suit the circumstances of the business.
4. The benefits of this approach are not limited to for-profit businesses. All organizations, including non-profits and governmental or quasi-governmental entities, can benefit from Top-Down Vision and Bottom-Up Management.

Exhibit 1.2

Allocation of a Leader's Energies in a TDVBUM Environment

The Ultimate Responsibility
Job number one

Developing and communicating a Vision that can lead a business to success is leadership's most important responsibility. Employees need and deserve the direction that comes from a clear Vision. It is the beacon against which they will measure their actions and decisions on a daily basis. Without this Vision, it is difficult to hold people accountable because they are lacking one of the most fundamental tools needed to achieve success – a clear understanding of the company's plan for its future.

Leaders should devote the largest portion of their time and energy to developing and communicating a Vision that will galvanize and inspire the entire organization. Conveying a clear and motivational Vision sets the business on the path to success. Jack Welch, one of the preeminent business leaders of the twentieth century supported this philosophy. He said, "Good business leaders create a vision, articulate the vision, passionately own the vision, and relentlessly drive it to completion."[1]

The remainder of the energy of a CEO or any other leader in the business should be primarily focused on the following activities:
- Listening to the feedback, suggestions and concerns of employees, customers, suppliers, stockholders and other stakeholders.
- Supporting (but not dominating) employees in their various endeavors. Example: Joining a salesperson on an important sales call, when asked. Supporting the sales presentation, where appropriate.

1. *Harvard Business Review*, Vol. 67 Issue 5, September-October, 1989.

- Coaching (but not directing) employees when they need or request guidance.
- Cheering and acknowledging employees when they make progress.
- Removing roadblocks to employee success.

Developing and communicating a Vision that can lead a business to success is leadership's most important responsibility.

Too few leaders commit sufficient time to these activities, instead devoting much of their energy to putting out the daily fires. They need to make a conscious effort to avoid becoming distracted by short-term crises or opportunities. Their role is to make sure the organization is focused on the Vision and that employees have the tools, resources, motivation, support and guidance to succeed.

While a Vision is the ultimate and defining responsibility of the CEO, it should not be created in a vacuum. It is important for the CEO and senior management to obtain input from mid-level managers and employees throughout the company. They can provide valuable insights because of their intimate knowledge of the workings of the company.

Painting a Picture
Glimpsing the future

The Vision for any business "paints a picture" of what it might look like at a future point in time. It provides an exciting and ambitious roadmap for people to follow and states why that goal is possible. It must inspire employees throughout the business to become creative participants in making the Vision a reality.

In 1966, Rollin King and Herb Kelleher developed a Vision on a restaurant napkin for a new airline that would eventually become dominant throughout the nation. The airline would be so attractive to people that they would fly rather than drive to locations three to eight hours away. King and Kelleher believed they could provide something missing in the industry: low costs and frequent flights that run on time with friendly service.

The Vision must describe where the business is heading and why it is likely to lead to success.

They planned to achieve the low costs by flying only one type of airplane (lower training and maintenance costs); by avoiding large inefficient hub airports; and by not serving meals (saving money and freeing space on planes for more seats). The low costs would facilitate extremely low fares, allowing them to dominate the routes they elected to serve, leading to more flights and higher ticket sales.

They planned to hire only people with a sense of humor who enjoy serving others. They figured that people-oriented and fun-loving flight attendants would enhance the experience for travelers. This classic Vision was a success formula that led

Southwest Airlines to become a multi-billion-dollar giant in the airline industry, one of the few airlines to be consistently profitable.

Too many businesses do not have a real Vision. Their management functions like generals who give the order to charge without telling the troops the direction. It is not necessary for leaders to know precisely how the company will turn its dream into reality, however. What is important when the Vision is developed is to instill confidence that the dream is attainable, even if it seems ambitious. The Vision takes into account a reasonable projection of the company's ability to develop or acquire the capabilities, technology or resources required to achieve the dream. True leaders are able to communicate inspiring Visions for their businesses and involve employees in making those Visions become reality.

On May 25, 1961, President John F. Kennedy made one of the great visionary statements of the 20th century: He committed the United States to landing men on the moon, and returning them safely, before the end of the decade. By painting this ambitious Vision, Kennedy galvanized the public and Congress to fund the space program. He equated success in this endeavor with status and self-respect as a nation and as a superpower. The inspiration and direction generated from Kennedy's Vision statement was, in many ways, just as important as NASA's role in developing the hardware, software and technologies to make Neil Armstrong's historic words from the moon ring out across the world.

How does a leader create a Vision that becomes the guiding light for a business? Is setting a Vision a fact-driven process or is it intuitive? In our experience, great business leaders artfully blend these two paths. As a start, it is very important for a leader to have an intuitive feel for the potential of the business and its future direction. To develop that into an effective, inspiring Vision and then transform the Vision into reality takes tangible skills, research, analysis and teamwork. Many of the specific steps needed are detailed in following chapters.

Surviving, Thriving or Diving
Seek downhill rides

Organizations thrive because they have Visions that guide them in the direction of success. They aim for–and reach–a position that allows them to accomplish their goals. The path is different for every business, but having a sound and shared Vision is essential to good leadership and organizational success.

Businesses that do not a have a shared Vision may thrive for a while. When conditions or circumstances change materially, however, they are often unable to anticipate and adjust to the new situation. If they have enough momentum, they might survive for some time, but in most cases, the lack of a shared Vision will cause the business to "dive" as it experiences distress. Proactive leadership can usually avoid this problem by developing a Vision for success and involving employees throughout the organization in determining how to accomplish it.

Biggest, by itself, is seldom a worthwhile goal.

Business success is really not that complicated. The businesses that provide products or services that people want, delivered in the fastest manner at the lowest real cost and highest-quality levels, are likely to succeed. The proviso is that the products or services must be sold at prices that generate adequate returns on their investment.

While this formula is easy to understand and appreciate, implementing it consistently over time can be daunting. The initial challenge, of course, is to predict the products and services customers will want. In fact, it is not easy to predict which customers will be best, let alone what products they will want, because of shifts in taste and demographics. Also challenging to predict are the technological changes that will affect demand, cost reduction, response time and opportunities for improvements in quality.

In the early 1990s, a Parkland client developed a cutting-edge approach to combining video, sophisticated software and unique hardware to develop interactive kiosks that would allow businesses to sell products and services in an unmanned format in public places. This enterprising strategy was overshadowed by the advent of the Internet shortly thereafter, which offered better access to customers at a fraction of the cost.

In spite of the difficulty of anticipating change, companies must constantly evaluate their environments. Businesses that stay abreast of emerging opportunities and threats and examine where they are heading are more likely to survive and thrive. They must constantly evaluate if and why their strategies are sound, taking into account all internal and external forces.

Change is normal in most industries and most businesses can make reasonably educated predictions about how things will change. Reality will not mirror those projections, but good internal and external intelligence pave the way for periodic minor course corrections that allow a business to adapt and respond effectively. The impact of some changes are relatively easy to predict, such as the changing demographics and related buying power of aging baby boomers. The most radical changes, such as the development of the Internet, are infrequent. These changes require more intense analysis and intervention.

Every business should seek to improve its market and financial position, looking for niches where it can differentiate itself from competitors and out-perform them. Biggest, by itself, is seldom a worthwhile goal. Instead, a company should aim to be the strongest, building competitive edges that allow it to outperform the competition. Nimbleness, flexibility and the ability to understand and respond to customers' needs will invariably trump brute force. Size is not necessarily a disadvantage, however. Some major companies (Wal-Mart, Southwest Airlines) have used their competitive edges to become large, but have maintained the ability to move ahead of competitors.

Successful businesses use competitive edges to dominate niches or micro-niches[1] that are worthwhile. They do not squander their resources on monumental efforts to dominate a shrinking industry, for example. Highly cyclical or risky industries also do not usually produce opportunities that make the risks acceptable. Choosing a Vision that favors niches that are not worthwhile is comparable to riding a bike uphill, when a downhill ride is equally available.

Successful businesses use competitive edges to dominate niches or micro-niches that are worthwhile.

Successful Visions invariably involve being the strongest and smartest competitor in a market that offers good opportunities. Most unsuccessful businesses charge ahead without adequate research. They soon discover there are stronger companies going after the same market share or, worse, the market is dwindling. No matter what efforts the companies make, they are doomed. Had they taken the time to examine where they were heading before tackling an uphill route, they might have been able to find a glorious downhill ride to a growing niche where they could thrive.

---

1.   A micro-niche is a specialized segment of a niche. For example, Callaway entered the golf equipment market by a specialized focus on drivers. Only when it had succeeded in dominating this micro-niche did it use its market position to expand into the broader golf equipment and clothing niches.

The "Aha!" Test
I get it

The objective of a Vision statement is to be inspirational: to motivate people throughout the organization to believe in the Vision and want to make it work. To achieve this, the Vision statement must convey to all employees *why it is likely to work* and how their contributions will be vital. After reading the Vision statement, most employees should react by saying, "I get it! I see how this Vision will lead our company to success and I want to be a part of this."

When crafting a Vision statement, leaders should constantly be asking themselves whether they believe it will pass this test. Over the past decade, many companies invested significant time and effort in writing mission statements. Many of these were recorded on posters that were prominently displayed throughout the business, reading something like: We will be the leader in our industry; our company will be a great place to work; we will be the low-cost producer; we will focus on customer satisfaction; and we will be a good corporate citizen.

he Vision must convey to all employees vhy it is likely to lead to success and how heir contributions will be vital.

While there is nothing wrong with these goals, they serve more as general philosophies and "feel-good" statements. They do not convey clear pictures of where the company is heading, how it will get there and why the plan is likely to work. It is unlikely that such vague statements will motivate employees.

In order to feel connected to the Vision, employees must be able to understand what role each individual will play in achieving it. The Vision must provide employees with guidance on how to take actions and make decisions on a day-to-day basis. In addition, it must communicate "what's in it for me" to employees. They should be able to understand the financial and non-financial benefits to them of achieving the Vision. The non-financial benefits (examples: self-esteem, responsibility, motivation, satisfaction, advancement, job security) are just as important as financial benefits, if not more so.

A strong Vision statement is inspiring, ambitious and convincing.

A strong Vision statement is inspiring, ambitious and convincing. It presents a focused plan for the future and reassures employees, shareholders, lenders and other stakeholders that the Vision is attainable – *and likely to lead to success.* If the Vision succeeds in these objectives, it can be the catalyst that spurs and guides the company to its desired success.

Leading to Success
Resist the "roll-up-the-sleeves" urge

The success of Top-Down Vision and Bottom-Up Management relies on the development of great ideas and highly effective implementation. Done well, the process unleashes the energy, motivation and talent of employees throughout the company. Good leaders create the right atmosphere by using their authority sparingly. Although they retain veto power for all major decisions, they focus their attention on developing employee talent and commitment to the Vision.

In a TDVBUM structure, managers must function as leaders. They guide people and provide resources and encouragement, rather than tell people specifically what to do. Leaders develop the Vision that will put the company on a path to success and prosperity, but they are willing to share responsibility for achieving the Vision with their teams.

True leaders motivate teams to pursue the Vision with energy and vigor. They are coaches and cheerleaders, guiding people when they stumble and hailing them when they succeed. This applies to all leaders in the company whether they are the CEO, a department head, supervisor, foreman, or team leader.

So many managers assume that because they have more power or experience, it is appropriate to give directives to employees. This trap must be avoided like the plague. Employees who are told what to do can become drones. Many, if not most, will faithfully try to execute the task as directed. The result: doing something the way it has always been done, relying solely on the manager's ability to generate improvements in the process.

Employees lose motivation as their problem-solving capabilities are dismissed and the dangerous not-invented-here syndrome kicks in.

In a TDVBUM structure, managers must function as leaders.

In our experience, effective leaders provide a broad outline for a task and work with an employee or a group of employees to establish commitment. Then the employee or team can develop a detailed plan to bring back for review. Employees who are told where the leader is trying to go and are asked to help figure out how to get there will usually work with a passion to find ways to achieve goals in the optimum manner.

A Parkland Group client in the ceramic tile industry experienced significant problems in shade variation in its production process. The result: excessive rejects, slow-moving inventory and dissatisfied customers. Because the problem was long-standing, the company accepted the consequences as a given in that industry.

When the CEO began his quest for a new Vision, he realized that a significant reduction in the shade variation was essential to the success of the business. Meetings were conducted with employees throughout the company to explain the importance of reducing shade variation and to solicit ideas. A cross-functional team was formed. Within weeks, the team generated numerous creative ideas that have since resulted in the number of shades declining from as high as 25 down to one or two. The benefit of these changes to the company and its customers has been immense.

Leadership encompasses many of the skills needed to be a good manager, but it goes a lot further. Managers primarily focus on supervising the execution of existing plans; leaders guide the development of plans and ensure they are effective and clearly understood. They remove the barriers to employee success, ensuring that their team members have the necessary skills, resources and infrastructure to succeed.

When an employee has performed poorly or made a mistake, the leader should always explore the cause. Was the problem a roadblock beyond the employee's control or inadequate training or communication? When problems are approached as learning experiences, the entire organization benefits. Employees will be willing to be creative in finding new and better ways to do their jobs, without fear of criticism.

An operator of a plastic injection-molding machine at a Parkland client was receiving constant criticism for her poor productivity. A team charged with improving productivity found that the molds being used were in poor condition and regular maintenance was not being done on the machine. Leadership training helped the department supervisor realize that he had not done a good job of removing the obstacles to the employee's success. The molds were sent out for repair and a regular preventative maintenance program was instituted for the machine, resulting in significantly improved productivity.

Employees who are told what to do can become drones.

It is always tempting for CEOs and other senior managers to involve themselves in details. Too many focus on strategies and tactics without ensuring that there is a shared Vision that will lead the company to success.

It is often comforting to roll up sleeves and "chip in" to help the company deal with its daily challenges. Successful leaders resist this temptation vigorously. Their job is to make sure the company has a winning plan. Getting involved in the details can dilute this effort and send a signal to employees that the buck does not stop with them. Nevertheless, it is appropriate and desirable for leaders to work alongside team members when leaders are coaching (not directing) or when they are building morale or demonstrating personal commitment.

Leaders remove the roadblocks to employee success.

Everything the leader says and does will be carefully scrutinized by team members looking for the truth and intentions behind the memos and speeches. Body language, actions and demeanor can often say more than pep talks. As noted professor and author Warren Bennis says, "A leader doesn't just get the message across – a leader is the message."

Being a leader requires understanding people. Effective leaders motivate people to reach higher and enjoy the process. Making the transition from manager to leader can be difficult. The CEO needs to set the example by being a good role model for the rest of the managers. Sometimes it is helpful for an organization to provide workshops and other training in critical leadership skills and group dynamics. The path to success is collaborative partnership, which must be supported in attitude as well as in structure.

20/20 Vision
Remove the blinders

Giving employees clear visibility into the company's plans and progress is essential for Top-Down Vision and Bottom-Up Management. Many business owners and managers have an unjustified fear of sharing sensitive information with their employees. Several issues usually drive this:

- Concern that employees might know too much about the owner's affairs, resent the prosperity that they learn about, or worry about the lack of prosperity as they become aware of it.
- Concern that employees are not qualified to understand the information and therefore might misinterpret it or jump to wrong conclusions.
- Fear that sharing information with employees might result in the data falling into the hands of competitors, resulting in adverse consequences for the company.

While these are legitimate concerns, the bigger issue is whether a business can succeed without providing information to employees that will allow them to help the company achieve its objectives.

Parkland recently consulted with a business that was losing a significant amount of money. When the CEO was asked if the senior executives of the business were aware of the financial condition, he said that although he had not shown them financial statements, he was sure that they were generally aware of the situation.

With the CEO's permission, at the next management meeting all

Exhibit 1.3

Information: Essential Ingredient

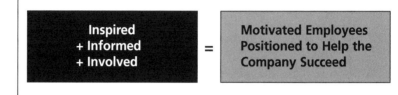

| Inspired + Informed + Involved | = | Motivated Employees Positioned to Help the Company Succeed |

the senior managers were asked to write on a piece of paper how they thought the company was doing. About half responded that the company was making a small amount of money, while the rest believed it to be breaking even.

Many business owners and managers have an unjustified fear of sharing sensitive information with their employees.

When the executives were shown the actual financial statements reflecting large losses, they all indicated that they would have conducted themselves very differently had they known the severity of the situation. Shortly afterward, a dramatic turnaround of the company began, in large part due to the employees of the company having a clear understanding of the challenge facing them.

If the employees of a business have not been thoroughly informed about the company's Vision and are not receiving regular and timely progress reports on how they are doing, their ability to achieve goals will be severely compromised. Accurate and timely information allows them to gauge their progress and make periodic course corrections.

Many employees are unfamiliar with accounting or other financial terminology, but information can be easily provided in a manner that is readily understandable to most people.

Graphs are often the best way to present information, showing actual performance against goals. Some companies use large "thermometers" which are adjusted daily. These solutions provide information in a way that is useful to employees, but meaningless to unauthorized outsiders.

It is important to share with employees the company's "drivers of success" (see Part II). These are specific elements of business performance that the company will focus on and measure to achieve success. Providing employees with regular updates on how these items are faring will greatly increase the probability of achieving the Vision.

Old data provides little value. Information should be shared on a timely and regular basis, preferably daily and weekly, to facilitate improvement. Mistakes and poor performance are discovered more quickly, facilitating timely corrective action. Just as important, successes can be celebrated sooner, helping to build morale.

A group of employees had been assembling a product used in the automobile aftermarket industry for several years. Throughout this time, they had worked at a steady pace, but were never aware of how satisfactory it was because they did not have a work standard. One of the Parkland Group's productivity specialists suggested to the group that they put up a flip chart in their work area to record their production rates every hour. The first hour they produced 105 units.

An employee suggested that they try to improve on that in the second hour. To their surprise, they produced 120 units without much additional effort. Enjoying their success, the group started to experiment with ways to speed up the process. Within two weeks, the group was consistently and proudly producing in excess of 200 units an hour, demonstrating the value of timely feedback.

Some of the most successful companies, such as GE, Southwest Airlines, Wal-Mart and Home Depot, have been very open about the secrets of their success. In fact, many CEOs either have written books about their methodologies or have cooperated with journalists and authors who have written about them. In reality, even if sensitive information were to fall into a competitor's hands, in most circumstances the damage that might result is minimal. The risk/reward ratio very often points to erring on the side of sharing information for companies that want to position themselves for ongoing success.

Old data is of little value. Information should be shared daily and weekly.

Most employees will make a genuine effort to help the company achieve its objectives if they understand and believe in the Vision and feel respected as valuable members of the team. Informing them about company performance or keeping them in the dark can make the difference between success and failure.

The True VIPs
Everyone is important

A hallmark of Top-Down Vision and Bottom-Up Management is the elimination of policies and practices that indicate to the organization that managers are more important than other employees. A successful business must be one team, with all members treated as vital contributors to success.

The leaders of an organization do bear more responsibility for the ultimate achievement of goals and results, but status should be derived from an individual's contribution, commitment and integrity – not his or her rank. All good leaders know that they will never achieve their objectives without the total cooperation and support of their team.

Because one weak link in the chain can jeopardize success, everyone's role is important. The success of superior products can be seriously undermined by a truck driver's lack of courtesy, a receptionist's abruptness or an engineer's lack of follow-through.

Leaders need to ensure that all employees are appreciated and treated with dignity and respect. This includes keeping team members in the loop of important communications, listening to their concerns and ideas, and recognizing their contributions and achievements, both in-house and externally.

Privileges of rank have long been synonymous with senior management in many businesses. Reserved parking spaces, executive dining rooms and other similar privileges drive a wedge between managers and employees. The TDVBUM methodology is built on the foundation of teamwork, which is not facilitated by these types of perks. Many of the best leaders genuinely believe that their team members are the true heroes who should be treated as VIPs.

Exhibit 1.4

The Buy-in Process

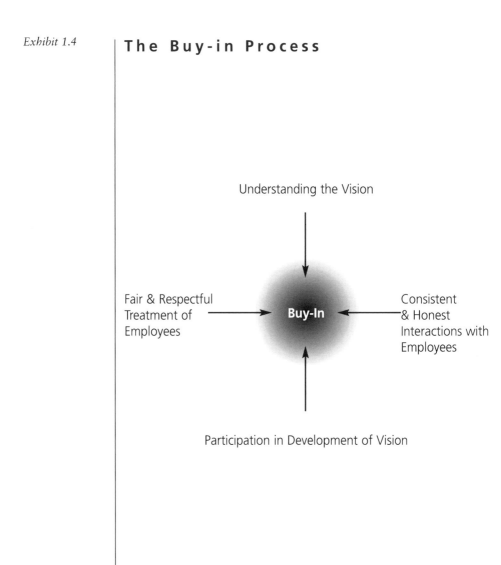

Buy-in
The catalyst for success

It is vital for the employees of a company to understand and commit to its Vision for the future. Achieving a consistent state of employee buy-in provides most businesses with a substantial competitive advantage. Getting to this state can be one of the least expensive and most valuable actions a business can take.

Businesses with great products, virtual monopolies, dynamic management and cutting-edge technology can easily fail to thrive, or even go out of business, if they do not succeed in mobilizing their employees. Committed, informed and empowered employees are the lubrication that makes the gears of a business function smoothly. These employees have the ability to create a path to success.

Employee buy-in for the corporate Vision is not hard to develop. An essential ingredient is trust, which does not come from well-written memos or impassioned speeches; it is the result of previous experiences. Businesses that have not been forthright with their employees in the past, or who have disregarded their input, will have to convince them that it will be different this time.

Buy-in is earned by consistent and honest interactions with employees, by keeping them informed, listening to their ideas and concerns and acting on them, treating them fairly and respectfully, and by allowing them to be involved in making the business better.

Sharing the Vision of the business with employees before it is cast in stone and asking for their views is one of the best ways to generate buy-in. It demonstrates respect for employees' capabilities, laying the groundwork for trust. Widespread buy-in can become the catalyst for all the actions needed to support business success. The company starts to become a motivated team with a shared Vision.

Businesses with great products, virtual monopolies, dynamic management and cutting-edge technology can easily fail to thrive, or even go out of business, if they do not succeed in mobilizing their employees.

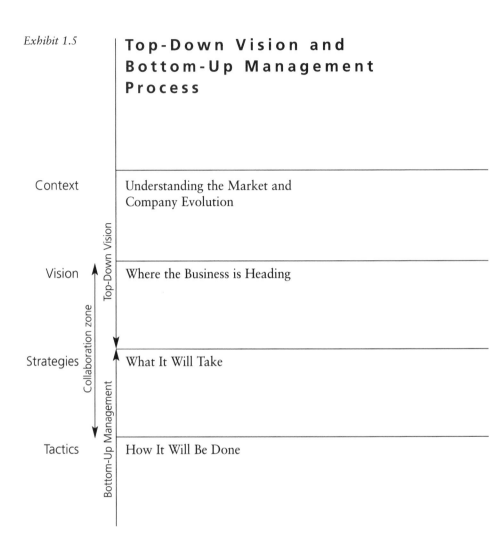

Exhibit 1.5

Top-Down Vision and Bottom-Up Management Process

Context	Understanding the Market and Company Evolution
Vision	Where the Business is Heading
Strategies	What It Will Take
Tactics	How It Will Be Done

Top-Down Vision

Bottom-Up Management

Collaboration zone

Overview of the Process
2+2=5

The Parkland Group has developed a specific process to develop and implement Top-Down Vision and Bottom-Up Management. This approach is relatively easy to implement, yet highly effective. Leaders and employees who participate in the process find it invigorating and satisfying and are invariably delighted with the results.

Leaders and employees who participate in the TDVBUM process find it invigorating and satisfying.

The TDVBUM process involves four distinct stages, the first two for Top-Down Vision and the remaining two for Bottom-Up Management. Exhibit 1.5 is a graphic representation of the Top-Down Vision and Bottom-Up Management process.

A. TOP-DOWN VISION

1. **Context – Understanding the company and market evolution:** Establishing a context before diving into the three main elements of the TDVBUM methodology is critical. The first step is an objective look at where the company and its industry are today. Then the marketplace should be examined and the future state of the industry projected.

2. **Vision – Where the business is heading:** A successful Vision describes the desired future state of the company in a manner that is clear, inspiring, ambitious and compelling.

B. BOTTOM-UP MANAGEMENT

1. **Strategy Development – What it will take to achieve the Vision:** The essential strategies for achieving the Vision are determined through a process of analysis that includes defining the factors that drive the company's success.

2. **Tactics – How the strategies will be implemented to achieve the Vision:** A comprehensive series of tactical plans are developed to support the strategies.

Subsequent chapters will deal with the details of each of the stages, with Top-Down Vision in Part I and Bottom-Up Management in Part II.

Exhibit 1.6

Top-Down Vision and Bottom-Up Management Process

Context

Top-Down Vision

Understanding the Market and Company Evolution

SWOT   Market Structure   Industry Evolution

Context
Understanding the market and company evolution

A good perspective of the internal and external conditions facing the business is a prerequisite to diving into the three main elements (Vision, Strategies and Tactics) of the Top-Down Vision and Bottom-Up Management methodology.

Setting a context is a two-part process. The first step requires an objective look at where the company and its industry are today; it is referred to as the "current state analysis." The next step is the "future state analysis," projecting how the industry is likely to evolve in the three to five years ahead. The future state represents the company's best estimation of how the industry might appear and what the marketplace will demand.

The combination of historical factual data and an educated projection of how the future will look form the context for developing an appropriate Vision for the future.

The senior management team usually does the future state analysis with input from customers, suppliers, trade groups, salespeople and other employees who might have a perspective on industry and market trends.

The combination of historical factual data and an educated projection of how the future will look form the context or basis for developing an appropriate Vision for the future. Several valuable analytical tools are used to assist in developing the knowledge that will be needed to construct the current and future state analyses.

SWOT Analysis

The simplest and most effective tool for assessing a company and the degree to which the external environment affects its performance is the battle-tested SWOT (Strengths, Weaknesses, Opportunities, and Threats) analysis framework. SWOT looks internally for a company's strengths and weaknesses. It also identifies those external opportunities and threats that are most likely to affect a business in the foreseeable future.

SWOT analysis identifies pointers for developing the ideal Vision; there are some general guidelines. When setting out to develop a company's Vision, it is beneficial to steer toward its *strengths*. If, for example, "Savvy Limited" is the technological leader in its field and it operates in a market that values technological advancement, it is logical to conclude that technological superiority should play an important role in its Vision.

Conversely, it is wise to aim away from segments that expose a company's *weaknesses*. If Savvy Limited is weak in sales and marketing, it could include in its Vision ways to go to market that compensate for those weaknesses. For example, it could form an alliance with another company with strong sales and marketing skills. If, on the other hand, Savvy determines that sales and marketing prowess are essential or strategic to its Vision, it may conclude that it needs to develop such skills in-house.

Creative brainstorming can identify and prioritize potential *opportunities*. Wayne Gretzky, the great hockey player, understood the importance of opportunity. He has said that the secret of his success was not focusing on where the puck was, but where it was going to be. Leveraging a company's strengths in an area of new and worthwhile opportunities can be the basis of a strong Vision. Imagine Savvy Limited using its technological expertise to lower the cost of its products. Currently limited to government and military markets, Savvy could then pursue more lucrative commercial applications.

Exhibit 1.7

Examples of Strengths & Weaknesses, Opportunities & Threats

Strengths	Clear competencies and capabilities Financial resources and balance sheet structure Strong customer relationships Proprietary knowledge or deep expertise Market share leadership Technology leadership Strong organization and structure Innovative marketing programs Strong reputation Distinct cost advantages Leadership and management strength

Weaknesses	Lack of strategic direction
	Poor strategic execution
	Lack of managerial depth and talent
	Lack of organizational effectiveness, functional expertise or
	    employee skills; knowledge and abilities are sub-par
	R&D capabilities not sufficient
	Inefficiency in operations
	Bloated cost structure
	Poor marketing programs
	Bad reputation in industry or with customers
	Insufficient financial resources to fund required activities to
	    remain competititve

Opportunities	Expand customer base beyond current segments Expand into new geographic or business markets Extend product offering to gain larger share of customer purchases Diversify into related services Fragmentation of industry Rapid market growth/expansion Weak competitors Technological advancement or alternatives Regulatory changes
Threats	Lack of entry barriers to new competition Slow market growth Regulatory changes Increased competitive rivalry Exposure to economic environment Shifts in demographic profile at customer level Changes in purchasing trends at buyer group level Technological advancement or alternatives

Exhibit 1.8

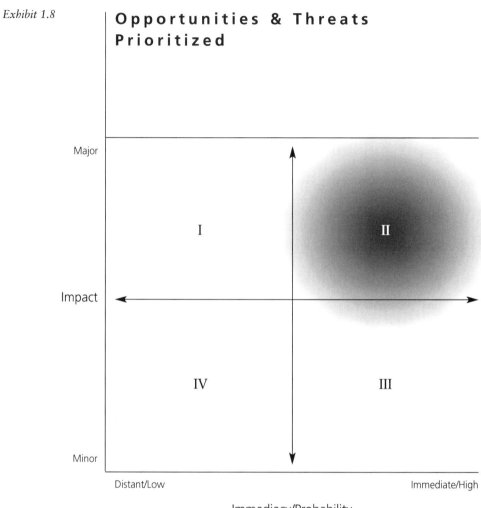

Opportunities & Threats Prioritized

Major

I   II

Impact

IV   III

Minor

Distant/Low   Immediate/High

Immediacy/Probability

Like weaknesses, *threats* must be identified, prioritized and evaluated in terms of immediacy, potential impact and level. Some threats can be avoided or circumvented with good planning and execution. The dangerous consequences of rising interest rates can be reduced significantly by hedging, for example. Other threats, such as a new competitor with superior-quality products, must be dealt with head-on to avoid disaster. Still others can be ignored or put on a back burner. Constantly analyzing potential threats allows strategy and tactics to be adjusted to meet the needs of the Vision.

By plotting the opportunities and threats on a 2x2 matrix like the one in Exhibit 1.8, they can be prioritized based on two criteria. On the horizontal axis, the immediacy of impact is charted and on the vertical axis, the degree of impact is identified. Items that are most critical in terms of their severity of impact and immediacy of impact will fall in quadrant II. These are the items upon which an organization will want to turn its focus and which will probably become areas of strategic attention. If an issue would have a severe impact in a short-time horizon, but has a low probability of being accomplished, then its relative priority is reduced compared to items with higher probabilities of becoming reality.

The process of completing a SWOT analysis can be complicated by the difficulty in determining whether something is a strength or a weakness, an opportunity or a threat. For example, is a powerful, dynamic, charismatic leader a strength because the organization responds to his/her compelling style? On the other hand, is it a weakness because the power of the leader's personality leaves little room for more than one idea at the top? Is the increasing power of 18- to 24-year-olds an opportunity because discretionary spending represents a higher portion of their total income? Alternatively, is it a threat because the life-cycle of purchasing trends among this group tends to be shorter than the more stable patterns of Baby Boomers? Analysis must be done with these types of potential conflicts in mind.

Market Structure Analysis

Understanding the structure of the markets is essential to context development. This analysis focuses on creating a picture of the external environment. It allows a business to look at suppliers, customers, the threat of new players entering the industry, the threat of substitute products and the intensity of

Exhibit 1.9

M a r k e t S t r u c t u r e A n a l y s i s: P o r t e r's F i v e F o r c e s

Threat of New Entrants – is low when:

- There is product differentiation
- Capital requirements are high
- There is limited access to distribution channels/customers
- There are restrictive government policies
- There is potential significant retaliation of incumbents
- There are economies of scale

Supplier Power – is greater if:

- Fewer suppliers or is more concentrated than the buying industry
- Supply product is differentiated or high switching costs
- There are few substitutes
- The buying industry is not an important customer of the supply industry
- Threat of forward integration exists

Rivalry – is intense when:

- Competitors are of similar size or power, or they are many in number
- Industry growth is slow
- Lack of product differentiation
- Capacity is augmented in large increments
- Capacity utilization is low
- Low switching costs
- Exit barriers are high
- Rivals are diverse in strategies

Buying Power – is high when:

- Customers are concentrated or buy in large volume
- Products are undifferentiated
- Products represent a large portion of customer's costs
- Customer earns low profits, creating incentive to drive costs lower
- The product is unimportant to the quality of the customer's product
- Switching costs are low
- Customer group poses a credible threat of backward integration

Threat of Substitutes – is high when:

- There is an abundance of products or services that serve the same function
- The price-performance trade-off of substitutes is attractive

Michael E. Porter "How Competitive Forces Shape Strategy," *Harvard Business Review*, March-April, 1979

current competition. Michael E. Porter[1] has written a great deal on this subject. His Five Forces analysis is an extremely valuable tool for analyzing market structure. (See Exhibit 1.9, Market Structure Analysis: Porter's Five Forces.)

Development and analysis of this information can be very helpful in steering a company's Vision down a path that increases the chances of success. For example, to be a buyer in a segment where supplier power is high (example: a monopolistic supplier) will generally be less desirable because of the control the vendor has over its customers. However, operating in a field where the threat of new entrants is low is attractive in most circumstances. If it is not easy for new competitors to enter the market, this is one less flank where the company must be vigilant.

Industry Evolution Analysis

Many books have been written about ways to develop strategic plans. Most of them do an effective job of giving guidance for dealing with what is known. Their effectiveness declines dramatically, however, when it comes to determining an accurate future state, which is necessary for an appropriate context for the Vision. Short of a time machine, how do we best achieve a better than 50 percent chance of predicting future events and trends?

To assist in this process, The Parkland Group uses a tool called Industry Evolution Analysis, which is designed to project a likely future scenario. First, we identify the key elements of the industry. Then we use the experience and knowledge of the company's leaders and employees to paint a picture of what the industry will look like in a three-to-five-year period.

This analysis examines numerous business characteristics. The past and present states, together with market intelligence and

---

1.   Michael E. Porter, "How Competitive Forces Shape Strategy," *Harvard Business Review*, March-April, 1979.

industry research, should put a company in a good position to predict what the industry might look like in the future.

For example, consider Retirement Villas, Inc., a business that develops real estate for retirees. Under the "Market Growth" characteristics, they might conclude the following:

Yesterday	–	*modest growth*
Today	–	*increasing*
Tomorrow	–	*rapid growth due to significant increase in retiring (and wealthy) baby boomers in the next five years*

In addition to market growth, the Industry Evolution Analysis also examines and considers the impacts of expected future trends in competition, profit margins, channels of distribution, power of vendors and buyers, manufacturing processes and technological developments. This analysis provides a business with a significantly better chance of accurately predicting the probable future changes in its industry.

Understanding the company's strengths, weaknesses, opportunities, threats, market structure and industry evolution provides a comprehensive context that forms the foundation or jumping-off point for developing an appropriate Vision.

Exhibit 1.10

Industry Evolution Analysis
Retirement Villas Inc.

Characteristics	Yesterday (Past Three to Five Years)	Today (Today's Environment)	Tomorrow (Three to Five Years Out)
Market Growth	Modest	Increasing	Rapid
Number of Competitors	Increasing	Substantial	Abundant
Profit Margins	Modest	High	Moderating
Foreign Competition	Low	Low	Slight increase
Channels	Primarily smaller to medium-sized developers	Migrating to larger developers	Very large, well-financed public company Developers will dominate
Power of Vendors	Ubiquitous	Ubiquitous	Higher-quality developments will compete for specialized talent
Power of Buyers	High	Moderating	Increasing competition for desirable properties
Manufacturing Process	Unsophisticated	Increasing sophistication	Highly efficient, focus on speed
Technological Developments	Very little	Increasing	Very important for lowering costs and satisfying tastes of sophisticated home buyers

Exhibit 1.11

Top-Down Vision and Bottom-Up Management Process

Context	Understanding the Market and Company Evolution

	SWOT	Market Structure	Industry Evolution

Vision

Where the Business is Heading

Vision Bias	Future Market Leader Profiled	Straw Man

Top-Down Vision

Vision
Where the business is heading

When the CEO and senior management have completed the context analysis, the process of creating a Vision may begin. The process involves defining the desired future state of the company in the context of its current state and the anticipated future state of the industry. The Vision developed collectively by the CEO and senior management can lead the company to success. Consequently, developing a compelling Vision is one of the most important functions of the leader of any organization.

A company's Vision represents the power of a beacon or guiding light.

To create a Vision there must first be a process of discovery. This includes understanding not only what the leader would like to see as an outcome, but also what values form the core of the connection between members of the organization. These values include moral values, risk tolerance, growth objectives, and attitudes toward colleagues, customers and community. Discovering what they are and how they work within the organization form part of the understanding needed to create the Vision.

To achieve the desired outcomes, a Vision must:
- Reflect the passion of the company's leader(s)
- Be ambitious
- Be researched well, tested and thought out
- Be achievable
- Be communicated effectively
- Reflect the values not only of those who construct it, but also of those who will bring it to life

- Have a time frame that is relevant to those responsible for achieving it
- Represent the power of a beacon or guiding light

Vision Bias

Most businesses bias their strategies to focus their competitive energies on a few areas. The six major biases that companies use to compete are:

Bias	Description
Cost	Consistently lower prices for customers
Service	Superior service and support
Quality	Superior product performance and reliability
Technology	Expertise and innovation that deliver products with better features and benefits
Distribution	Sales and marketing muscle that give customers easier and better access to products and services
Style	Products or services that look or feel better to customers

When developing its Vision, a business should ask itself which biases it has focused on in the past. (What biases have allowed it to reach its present state?) To do this, it should rank the six areas of bias, starting with the most dominant one.

For example, Wal-Mart might rank itself in the following manner:

1. **Cost**–*The entire organization is structured for consistently lower costs for its customers.*

2. **Distribution**–*Its goal is to blanket the country and eventually the world with its stores, providing easy access and one-stop shopping for customers.*

3. **Service**–*Wal-Mart's employees are very friendly and go out of their way to serve customers.*

4. **Quality**–*It strives to ensure that products meet customers' needs.*

5. **Technology**–*Wal-Mart does not compete based on its technological prowess, but it does use technology very successfully to help drive down costs. Its information systems technology and inventory tracking/moving technology are important strengths.*

6. **Style**–*Because Wal-Mart is a retailer of predominantly basic products, style is not emphasized in the appearance of its stores or its products.*

Contrast this to Apple Computer:

1. **Style**–*In the past, style was important to Apple, but it also placed a lot of emphasis on product superiority. With the introduction of the very visually appealing iMac product, style appears to be edging out technology.*

2. **Technology**–*Apple's rise was primarily built on the superiority of its operating system over Windows.*

3. **Quality**–*With its customers typically sophisticated users, quality is important.*

4. **Service**–*While service is important to every organization, it is not a major competitive bias for Apple.*

5. **Cost**–*Apple's customers do not generally buy its products because of price.*

6. **Distribution**–*Apple has never been able to match its major competitors on distribution.*

When developing its Vision, the senior leadership of a business should also explore:

- Whether the biases focused on in the past served the business well
- If those biases will lead the business to its goals in the future
- If the biases need to be changed
- Why the future bias will be likely to lead to success

It frequently happens that the bias that a company "brought to the dance" is not the one it wants to go home with.

A Parkland client in the lighting industry built a respectable position in the market by being the technological leader in its field. However, whenever it developed a good and popular product, its larger and more efficient competitors would copy the product and take away its market share. When the technology curve started to flatten out, its technological advantage became less valuable. The company changed its bias toward cost to retain its market share.

It frequently happens that the Vision

that a company "brought to the dance"

is not the one it wants to go home with.

Decisions on bias are central to a company's definition of itself and its Vision. When a company has determined what bias priorities serve it best, its Vision becomes substantially clearer.

Future Market Leader Profiled

From the understanding of market structure and the prioritized opportunities and threats (see Context chapter), it is possible to begin defining the future market leader. This is the hypothetical competitor who, given the assumptions about the future, is likely to dominate the market in the future. This is the competitor that all of the other players in the market will fear – and the company that successful companies should strive to be.

The future market leader can be profiled by analyzing the business system and defining what the future market leader's strengths will be at each level of the system. The resulting profile provides a benchmark to evaluate where the firm stands relative to the future market leader's strengths. This profile allows the company to identify the gaps between its current state and the future market leader, as well as what it would take to fill the gaps. (See Exhibit 1.12: Future Market Leader Profile Example & Gap Analysis.) This profile of a hypothetical market leader should provide a solid target for the company's Vision.

Exhibit 1.12

Future Market Leader Profile Example & Gap Analysis
Power Tool Manufacturing, Inc.

	Future Market Leader	Gap Fillers
Product Development	Cutting-edge design and enhancements New products are 10% of annual revenue	Need to develop or outsource capability to design and develop innovative new product entries
Procurement	Best sourcing of prices and vendor partnerships	Improvements in supply chain management (pricing, terms, JIT)
Mfg/Assembly	Best use of in-house and outsource activities (highly efficient) High level of automation and productivity Focus on continuous improvement	Improved work flow and reduced turn-over in assembly area
Sales/ Marketing	Best-in-class point of sale merchandise and re-seller programming Top-of-mind awareness within target groups Maximize shelf presence in all three outlet types	Need to develop capabilities to manage the shelf and merchandising requirements at big box reseller Sales force developed to effectively manage target channels and categories
Distribution & Logistics	Cost leadership, top quartile of delivery accuracy, timing, quality – all channels	Need to develop capability to manage smaller, shorter lead-time delivery requirements of high-velocity reseller initiatives
Customer Service	Ability to service both retail and wholesale segments at high levels	Need to develop automated order and custom management systems Upgrade training and development programs for CS personnel
Support Function (MIS, Finance, HR)	*Highly efficient IT and communication systems, timely management information, efficient and effective recruiting and mangement training programs, self-directed work teams, empowered workforce*	*Invest in more efficient and effective IT solutions and infrastructure* *Increase empowerment and teamwork* *Increased focus on management training and development*

Straw Man

The process of creating a Vision does not work the same way in all companies. The CEO may take the output from the context analysis and start with his/her draft of a Vision. Sometimes the senior executives will work together as a team to develop the Vision. In other cases, the CEO, either individually or with the leadership team, will amend an existing Vision. Whatever the process, employees from a cross-section of the enterprise (functions and levels) must be involved in providing feedback in brainstorming sessions and other meetings on the Vision that senior management develops.

An effective technique for developing the Vision is for the CEO to draft a "straw man" or proposed conceptual Vision statement. This should be presented to the senior management team for its input and modification. It should then be presented to employees throughout the company, who should be given ample opportunity to understand, discuss and comment on it. This invariably generates input that improves the Vision and helps employees feel connected to the process. The Vision should not be finalized until it has been through this process.

Employees from a cross-section of the enterprise (functions and levels) must be involved in providing feedback on the Vision that senior management develops.

While a Vision statement should be written to stand the test of time, it must be reviewed periodically to ensure that the Vision remains consistent with the current context. In all cases, the CEO and the senior management team must describe what the business might look like in the future, taking into account its current context and the likely marketplace and industry evolution. The Vision will represent their dream for the business.

Exhibit 1.13

Vision Statement Components Template

Vision Summary	*An overview statement summarizing the desired future state of the organization*			
	People/ Culture	**Operations**	**Customers/ Markets**	**Finance**
Vision Elements *Where the Business is Heading*	• Skills • Culture • Work Environment	• Cost • Quality • Responsiveness • Innovation	• Markets Served, Products Offered • Customers Targeted • Value Proposition/ Reason to Thrive	• Growth Rates • Profitability Targets • Capital Structure • Return on Investment

Components of the Vision Statement
The specifics

Oone of the biggest dilemmas for leaders is determining what form the Vision statement should take – which aspects of the future need to be defined. Although every business is different, several elements should be included in all Vision statements. These elements provide guidance to leaders and employees as they plan for and react to the issues, opportunities and problems they encounter on a day-to-day basis. With this guidance, it is easier to make decisions that consistently lead a business down the path to its desired goal.

Although every business is different, all Vision statements should address people/culture, operations, customers/markets and finance.

The Vision statement is broken down into two important parts:

- **Vision summary:** An overview statement summarizing the desired future state of the organization in no more than 30 words. The Vision summary, at a minimum, briefly describes the company's future products, services and markets as well as how it will compete and grow.
- **Vision elements:** Describes the desired future state in detail, encompassing the four major elements of business activity. (For a typical Vision statement, see Exhibit 1.14.)

Vision Elements

1. **People/Culture:** The people, skills, work environment, culture and organizational structure that will be needed to achieve the Vision.

The culture and camaraderie of a business greatly influence its ability to achieve its Vision. The skills and personality profiles of the employees that the company will require to achieve the Vision must be defined. In addition, the Vision statement should clearly express how the company feels about its people, its community, ethics, integrity and other non-financial, but vitally important, cultural issues.

Southwest Airlines is a company that has very clearly defined its Vision as it relates to people and culture. It strives to hire fun-loving employees who enjoy serving people and working in a team environment with a minimum of bureaucracy. This clarity of Vision has been a major part of Southwest's success.

Enron, on the other hand, seemed to look for people who could help the company grow at a rapid rate. This priority placed a higher value on profits than customer satisfaction or integrity and appears to have played a significant role in the company's downfall.

Authority, responsibility and other similar organizational structural issues should be addressed to provide clarity about roles, expectations and accountability.

2. **Operations:** The company's Vision with regard to the cost and quality of its products and services, as well as its ability to be responsive to customers' needs, must be defined. The company's approach to innovation should also form part of the Vision statement.

Some businesses strive to be the lowest-cost producer in their industries. Some emphasize being premium-quality suppliers and do not compete on price. Other businesses may strive to be exceptionally responsive; for example, they may offer same-day service or a broad range of cus-

Exhibit 1.14

Vision Statement
Solid Construction Company

Vision Summary	*To be the preferred construction manager of commercial buildings in southwest Florida for customers who seek unique, high-quality structures.*

	People/ Culture	Operations	Customers/ Markets	Finance
Vision Elements	• Collaborative • Team-based • Ethical • Customer satisfaction #1 priority	• Meets deadlines • Rapid response to customers' needs • Efficient • High quality at reasonable cost • Daily computerized cost & progress controls	• Products: office bldgs., cultural & recreational facilities • Customers: large corps., larger cities & institutions • Markets: Sarasota to Naples • Reason to thrive: ability to recruit & manage sub-contractors that can do quality, timely, & unique work at reasonable costs	• 20% annual revenue growth • 6% EBIT • Debt/Equity <2:1

tomized options. These Vision goals may require adjustments in operational infrastructure.

The contrast between fast-food restaurants and fine-dining restaurants illustrates the differences in operational vision. The speed and consistency required in a McDonald's outlet dictates a very different approach from the emphasis on taste and ambience of a gourmet restaurant. The Vision statement provides the direction and guidance for the development of the operations strategy.

Sample Operational Vision Statements:

Fast Food – Limit customer waiting time (including in line) to four minutes. Discard food not sold within thirty minutes. Limit quality complaints to less than two percent. Food cost below thirty percent.

Fine Dining – Seat patrons with reservations within five minutes of arrival. Greeting by waiter/drink order within three minutes of seating. Entrée served within twenty-five minutes of order. Quality complaints less than five percent.

3. **Customers/Markets:** The Vision statement must clearly state where and how the company intends to compete.

Definition of the business and products
The company's future business functions may not be the same as current ones. Guidance should be given about products, services, likely geographic expansion/contraction and distribution channels.

The Vision responds to the unique circumstances and objectives of a specific business.

Although Amazon.com started as an on-line retailer of books, its Vision included plans for a much wider range of products, including electronics, toys, housewares and computers. Knowing this information placed employees in a stronger position to develop and implement marketing and operational strategies and tactics.

Target customers
Determining target customers is an important element of a Vision Statement. While it is always tempting to try to serve all potential customers, success is easier to achieve if

a business focuses on satisfying the needs of the customers who fit the Vision.

Wal-Mart has focused its business strategy on serving lower-to-middle-income customers. Target, on the other hand, has aimed at more upscale customers. While pursuing different customers, both have been very successful at providing the merchandising and service that appealed to the targeted audience. This clarity of Vision as it related to customers has been a significant factor in the success of these companies.

Value Proposition

The value proposition defines what the company is offering to customers that creates enough value to warrant their parting with money in exchange. This definition is an assumption about what customers value.

In the case of Southwest Airlines, the value proposition is for the traveler to pay a bit more than alternative means of transportation (bus, train, rental car, or own car) would require to fly short-haul routes on bare-bones planes with minimal service. The benefit: expedited travel. This arrangement is of value only to those for whom in-flight refreshments, assigned seats and non-stop flights to most destinations are not important.

On British Airways, the value proposition is to pay somewhat more than the competition charges to have a luxurious, comfortable, no-hassle flight with every conceivable in-flight amenity made available. These two propositions are of value to two very different customer profiles and each has proved to be a valid hypothesis.

Reasons to Thrive

It is essential to develop competitive advantages, which allow a business to survive and thrive over the long haul. One of the most fundamental competitive advantages is protection by law: a patent. Drug companies are one example of businesses that have enjoyed tremendous benefits from patents.

For those businesses that do not enjoy the advantage (albeit temporary) afforded from patents and other similar legal protections, other competitive advantages exist. These include technology (Microsoft), reliability (Maytag), speed of turnaround (Dell), lower costs (Wal-Mart), status (Lexus) and service (Nordstrom).

Employees can also be a competitive advantage. By taking special measures to hire, motivate and train people who have or can develop unique skills or attributes, businesses can turn their employees into one of the most effective and powerful competitive advantages available.

4. **Finance:** The last important element of a Vision Statement defines the financial goals and direction the business is pursuing. This encompasses the desired growth rates, profitability targets and capital structure.

Growth rate
While it is always relatively easy to put a spreadsheet together that predicts tremendous growth for a business, in practice it is hard to forecast with any accuracy the size of a business several years into the future. However, the CEO does need to make it clear whether the business is planning to grow modestly or significantly. If growth will be part of the future of the company, the Vision must describe the general direction for such growth.

Knowing the approximate planned growth rate allows managers and employees to consider ideas and actions in the appropriate context. Strategies that may be very reasonable in a high-growth strategy could appear reckless in

> *It is essential to develop competitive advantages, which allow a business to survive and thrive over the long haul.*

a stable environment.

When Bernie Marcus started The Home Depot, he made it clear that they intended to grow the company very rapidly. Knowing from the beginning that they would need the systems, infrastructure and people to facilitate rapid growth allowed managers and employees to implement strategies and tactics to accommodate the growth.

Profitability

All Vision statements should provide guidance about the profitability and returns that will be expected from the business. This information will enable managers and employees to make effective decisions regarding capital investments, expenses, profit margins and pricing.

Capital Structure

After a business has determined its desired growth and profitability rates, it determines how it will finance the business to accommodate such goals. The plan should define the sizes and sources of capital, including accounts payable, debt and equity capital.

When all the elements of the Vision have been developed, the leaders and employees of a business should have a very clear idea of where the business is heading in all of the major elements of People/Culture, Operations, Customers/Markets and Finance. They are then in an excellent position to start working on the strategies that will be needed to achieve the Vision.

Exhibit 1.15

Top-Down Vision and Bottom-Up Management Process

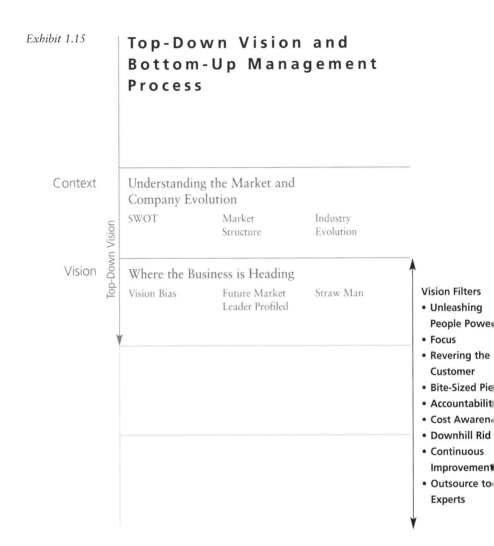

Context

Understanding the Market and
Company Evolution

SWOT   Market   Industry
         Structure   Evolution

Vision

Where the Business is Heading

Vision Bias   Future Market   Straw Man
         Leader Profiled

Top-Down Vision

Vision Filters
- **Unleashing People Power**
- **Focus**
- **Revering the Customer**
- **Bite-Sized Pie**
- **Accountability**
- **Cost Awareness**
- **Downhill Ride**
- **Continuous Improvement**
- **Outsource to Experts**

Vision Filters
Staying on the path

To give a Vision statement a good chance of success, it is helpful to provide guiding principles to use in making decisions and plans. These filters help evaluate whether specific actions fit the path the business wishes to follow. All decisions contemplated should be checked against the following filters:

Unleashing people power
An inspired, informed and involved workforce is key to sustained success. Any proposed actions that do not support and enhance this state should be reevaluated wherever possible.

Focus
A well-defined Vision allows a business to evaluate and prioritize options, focusing all resources on meeting its goals. A tight focus allows a business to master its craft, developing the knowledge and skills to excel.

One of the most prevalent causes of business failure is the dangerous grass-is-greener syndrome. Businesses usually start out with a reasonably focused strategy. As time passes, the original core business may not be performing as well as management would like, causing it to covet a diversification strategy that appears attractive. Expansions of the strategy can range from wider product ranges to vertical integration to completely diverse new ventures.

Management often finds that the expansion is not as attractive as it seemed from the outside looking in. The learning curve often requires spending substantial time and resources (including capital) on the new opportunity. The result? The original core focus frequently becomes starved for attention and funds, developing problems that are even more serious.

A Parkland client inherited ten gas stations from his father. While not a particularly exciting business, it did generate a steady, if not large, profit. Feeling the need to grow and "make his mark" on the business, the son decided to sell gas and lubricants on a wholesale basis to municipalities and industrial customers. He soon discovered that although the products were the same, the terms, conditions and profitability of the wholesale business were significantly less attractive than the retail business. The lack of focus seriously jeopardized his original business. By the time he was able to extricate the company from this new venture, it had lost significant amounts of money.

Revering the customer[1]

Very few businesses will have lasting success if they are not totally committed to placing customer satisfaction as the company's highest priority All actions planned by a business should be put through the customer satisfaction filter to ensure that customers are not treated as "wallets with people attached." Profit should be considered a by-product of customer satisfaction. Profits will be sustainable if satisfaction is the goal and is created efficiently.

All decisions contemplated should be checked against the Vision filters to ensure that the business stays on the Vision's path to success.

A focus on profits that takes precedence over customer satis

---

1. Revering the customer is the second foundation of a turbocharged company, described in *The Turbocharged Company*, Goddard and Brown, York, 1995.

faction can cause a company to take shortcuts that might improve short-term profits, but negatively impact long-term profits and even viability. Consider a situation where a business decides to use cheaper (and inferior) components in its product that are not visible to the customer, but that could affect the longer-term durability of the product. The company's profits will improve for a while, but its credibility could be dealt an irreparable blow when the product fails.

Bite-sized pieces

Taking one step at a time is the way to reach a destination in a journey. Similarly, breaking tasks down into smaller tasks that people can understand and manage effectively helps them complete tasks faster and more efficiently. Bite-sized tasks appropriate for the circumstances and skill levels of the people involved have significantly greater chances of being successfully accomplished.

Accountability

Very few plans will come to fruition without holding people accountable for results. Greater degrees of ownership and pride evolve when people know that a particular task is their responsibility and they will answer to their colleagues if goals are not met and will be favorably acknowledged if they are.

In order to achieve accountability, it is vital to give employees authority as well as responsibility. All the best intentions can be thwarted by the inability to carry out necessary actions. The person or team given the responsibility for a task must have appropriate control over all of the key elements of the task.

Consider a situation where a team is given responsibility for developing and launching a new product by a certain date. It is able to control all phases of the program except manufacturing of the product, which is done by a different division. If manufacturing does not produce on time, the team is powerless to meet its deadline.

In all but the smallest businesses, processes are usually suffi ciently complex to make it impractical for employees or ever teams to have direct span of control over the complet process. As a result, the organization needs to establish mech anisms for indirect span of control.

The most effective form of indirect span of control is an inter nal customer/vendor structure. Under this environment th next downstream process (whether an internal or externa process) is treated as a customer. The upstream "vendor" i accountable to the downstream customer for quality, deliver and cost. This structure can provide very effective span of con trol even in complex environments.

Very specific goal timelines for individuals and teams are essen tial for true accountability. Regular progress reports against sucl goals further enhance the effectiveness of the accountability.

Cost awareness, measurement and control

It is pure folly to embark on a venture without good cos information and the ability to control, measure and manag costs. All plans and strategies should be put through a cost fil ter to ensure that the appropriate systems and controls will b in place. Part III (Real Accounting), Tool 3 provides a discus sion on activity-based costing, the method we advocate fo determining the true cost of a product, activity or process.

Downhill ride

Certain factors, such as growth markets, barriers to entry, o high switching costs enhance the probability of success for ; company. However, businesses should generally avoid goin; against dominant competitors. Even if a market is growing, i there are entrenched companies effectively dominating tha market, it will be significantly harder for a new entrant to b successful. It is wise for businesses to pick segments that offe easier routes to success. Slogging up a treacherous hill is nc desirable in business, especially if there is an alternate downhill path to success.

Continuous improvement

Whatever direction a business pursues, all of its actions should be set up to encourage, expect, measure and reward continuous improvement in every area of the business. Its culture should be to strive to improve regardless of current levels of skill or superiority. Even if a business is the leader in its field, it should assume that someone is developing and implementing a plan to overtake it. The continuous improvement mentality should permeate the entire company.

Very few businesses will have lasting success if they are not totally committed to placing customer satisfaction as the company's highest priority.

Outsource to experts

There is often a temptation in business to do too much and "be all things to all people." Many managers derive comfort from having total control over the complete process. However, many companies perform tasks that could easily be performed by others that have greater expertise, better machinery or lower costs. Unless direct control over such processes is essential for strategic or quality control purposes, it is usually best to contract out such activities and have the company focus its efforts on what it does best.

Follow the Leader
Taking your cue

Vision is not only the CEO's task; it is the responsibility of every leader in an organization. The CEO and the senior leaders of the company set the overall Vision and direction. All other leaders in the business must translate the company's Vision into Visions for their divisions, departments, teams or groups. These mini-Visions must be consistent with the company's Vision, and must provide guidance for team members on where they are heading and what part they play in the overall direction of the business.

Consider the Vision summary of Manuprod Engineering Company: "To become the best manufacturing consulting firm in the Midwestern United States." A key to this was a Vision component to recruit and retain bright, flexible and highly motivated people with extensive manufacturing experience.

Vision is not only the CEO's task; it is the responsibility of every leader in an organization.

Manuprod's vice president of Human Resources formed a team to help develop an appropriate Vision for their department that would allow the company to achieve its goal. The Vision they developed was: "To develop the recruiting, motivation, compensation and career advancement systems and methods that will consistently demonstrate Manuprod's respect and appreciation for talented people who strive to be part of an exciting and successful team."

In a Top-Down Vision and Bottom-Up Management environment, a person can be a team member and a leader at the same time, depending on the Vision level. These changes in roles require different behavior to fit the circumstances.

Manuprod's Human Resources vice president was a member of the CEO's Executive Leadership Team that participated in the development of the company's overall Vision. In that role, she functioned as a Bottom-Up manager, providing feedback and input to her leader about his Top-Down Vision.

When she established the Vision development team in the Human Resources department, she played a very different role, becoming the leader who proposed a "straw-man" Vision for the department. In this role, she was the one receiving the "Bottom-Up" feedback and input from the team.

First, a company develops a Vision that communicates its direction to the entire company. Then this Vision is translated into interlocking mini-Visions for all parts of the business, achieving a state of "shared Vision."

Verify the Vision
Avoiding "Ready, Fire, Aim"

Before a Vision is rolled out to an organization for full-scale implementation of Bottom-Up Management, there is a critical need for verification of all aspects of that Vision. The verification process must ensure that the Vision is relevant, appropriate and likely to succeed. A good idea that is ahead of its time, subject to technical or regulatory hurdles, targeted at the wrong customers or subject to fierce competition will probably fail.

The verification process must ensure that the Vision is relevant, appropriate and likely to succeed.

Many ideas initially deemed attractive, even exciting, are discovered upon execution to be flawed by something truly unforeseen or poorly assessed. Examples of these fatal flaws may be problems such as a product being too costly, not convenient enough or not sufficiently in demand.

The original Vision of the superliner Titanic was that a large, high-speed, safe ocean liner operating on schedule would provide safety and value to the languishing ocean travel industry. The result would be an increase in demand. Unfortunately, numerous weaknesses were not addressed in the enthusiasm for the uniqueness of the Vision. Among these was the fact that the large passenger capacity became a setup for a major disaster in an accident that required lifeboats for everyone on a ship that had no room to store adequate numbers of them. The high speed and adherence to schedule sealed the fate of the Titanic when large icebergs were encountered.

How does a business leader go about verifying the Vision concept so that the organization can move forward confidently? The members of the senior management team are vital to testing the Vision. They are the first and, perhaps, the most useful sounding boards for the Vision. A process of brainstorming with this senior management team commonly results in considerable fine-tuning of the initial concept. The probability of success increases as questions and concerns are raised about the merits of the Vision and the feasibility of its implementation. Trade-offs are considered as the concept is honed into a practical Vision that is likely to succeed.

Once the buy-in of the senior management team has been achieved, the opinions of other constituents need to be taken into account. At this stage, it is very helpful to seek the input and feedback from an employee advisory team, if one has been formed. (See Bottom-Up Management: Types of Teams.) This cross-functional team, made up of people from various functions and levels throughout the company, can provide valuable insights and feedback that are instrumental in determining the viability of the proposed Vision.

It is likely that a sound assessment process will create new questions about the Vision.

Selected customers can also be important sources of Vision verification. These customers should be asked, "Is this an idea that will be of value to you?" and "What are the barriers to its success?" Other constituents, such as industry observers and commentators, key suppliers and outside experts can also be canvassed to glean additional insights.

It is likely that a sound assessment process will create new questions about the Vision. It should serve as an opportunity to reflect upon issues addressed in the context development process and may provide insights about the Vision's market impact, the anticipated response of competitors and potential barriers to success.

Vision statements should be developed based on a thorough analysis of data and facts that support direction. Plans based on "gut" feelings are less likely to be realized. Targeting a new market segment that is verified by extensive market research is an example of a fact-and-data-based Vision.

With all this feedback, the CEO and the senior management team are equipped with information that increases their confidence in the Vision or allows them to modify the Vision to increase the probability of its success. The CEO needs to have a high degree of confidence in the Vision before rolling it out to the entire organization.

The Vision verification process should be put on a fast track, to ensure the priority of resource allocation and the timeliness of test data. The senior management team needs to be intimately involved to guide the process and be confident of the adequacy of the results. Vision verification may involve building a business model prototype or running field trials, using the concept to gather test data.

The transition to the completion of a Vision summary and the Vision elements (see Components of the Vision) should be accomplished only when the Vision concept is determined to be feasible and likely to lead the company to success. If done well, the verification process can provide that confidence, backed by a healthy level of scrutiny throughout the entire TDVBUM process.

Part II

Bottom-Up Management

"Listen to the man who works with his hands. He may be able to show you a better way to do it."

Louis I. Kahn
Architect

Tilt the Playing Field
Unleashing people power

The competitive business world is an arena where playing on a level field is not rewarded. The name of the game is to be the best you can be and consistently outperform your competitors. In recent years, some companies have begun to recognize the potential of tapping the full capabilities of their employees. They understand that people are more energized and creative when they are informed about the company and given an opportunity to participate in the thinking side of the business.

When employees are invited to use their heads along with their hands, they will throw their hearts and souls in with the package, at no additional cost to the company. The result is that enlightened companies engage most of their competitors in a fight that is not "fair" because they have turned their employees into their best competitive advantage.

Employees usually have a better awareness than management of the grass-roots issues and challenges in the business.

The Parkland Group has worked with many businesses that have made this transition. We always enjoy seeing the "people power"[1] that is unleashed. Some people who were previously considered by management (and, in some cases, even themselves) to be relatively ordinary raise their performance several notches, transforming themselves from followers into leaders.

1. "People Power" is the first foundation of a turbocharged company, described in *The Turbocharged Company*, by Goddard and Brown, York, 1995.

Inspiring, informing and involving people at all levels costs virtually nothing, other than some time and effort in training them to think and behave in a different manner. Contrary to what people might think, this does not take an inordinate length of time and, in most cases, the costs are reasonable.

Most people take to this change like ducks to water. For the first few weeks, there is some uncertainty and hesitation because it is a new experience and people are skeptical about management's sincerity. However, provided management clearly and consistently demonstrates its commitment, in most situations employees will soon enthusiastically support the approach, roll up their sleeves and start contributing.

When employees are invited to use their heads along with their hands, they will throw their hearts and souls in with the package.

Employees who are responsible for day-to-day execution of the company's operations on the factory floor, in the warehouse, in the office and in sales are intimately familiar with the business. They usually have a better awareness than management of the grass-roots issues and challenges in the business. This invariably puts them in a strong position to develop appropriate creative ideas and solutions. They have a wealth of knowledge about how to make things function more efficiently because they work with them every day.

Including mid-level managers and all employees in the process of determining how to turn a dream into reality unleashes two powerful forces: ownership and teamwork. Instead of a series of directives issued from the top to a somewhat disinterested group of employees, there is a joint effort of leaders and employees at all levels working together to implement the Vision. Allowing employees to be involved in this manner is "Bottom-Up Management."

Two Heads Are Better Than One
The power of teams

Enlightened businesses have discovered that allowing employees to use their heads as well as their hands is one of the most important keys to success. Truly successful companies have learned that allowing employees to use their intellectual powers in a team-based format is even more powerful. It offers the potential for quantum leaps in business effectiveness.

Working in teams,[1] the strengths and talents of all team members can be drawn out via group dynamics. Any individual's weaknesses can usually be compensated for by the strengths of other team members. Most teams are able to develop ideas and plans that are far superior to those that are developed by individuals. Teams also make people feel better about their jobs and the company because they provide a sense of involvement, belonging and self-worth. Important additional benefits are the opportunity for employees to learn from each other and improved communications in the organization.

Most teams are able to develop ideas and plans that are far superior to those that are developed by individuals.

1. Care should be exercised to ensure that teams are not deemed "labor organizations" under the National Labor Relations Act ("NLRA"). Employee committees (or teams) that deal with employers concerning grievances, labor disputes, wages, rates of pay, hours of employment or conditions of work can be deemed to be labor organizations under the NLRA. Under this Act, the company can be held responsible for an unfair labor practice if it is determined that management has dominated or interfered with the formation or administration of any labor organization. As such, teams should not become involved in the above activities, and expert legal advice should be obtained if there is any doubt or concern.

Traditional organizations are set up with functional departments specializing in one particular aspect of the process, such as scheduling, work order sub-assembly, assembly or shipping. Departments, also known as silos, tend to function autonomously. They complete their tasks and then pass the process, product or paperwork to the next department. Communication within each department is primarily vertical, with bosses or supervisors issuing directives in primarily a top-down format. Communication between departments is often minimal or strained. Information and span of control are confined to small parts of the business. Employees in these silos are generally only exposed to the activity in their areas, with little involvement in, or concern for, the activities that take place before or after them.

Exhibit 2.1

T r a d i t i o n a l   B u s i n e s s   P r o c e s s   a n d   I n f o r m a t i o n   F l o w

Most communication within departments is top-down. Communication between departments is minimal and "tossed over the silo wall."

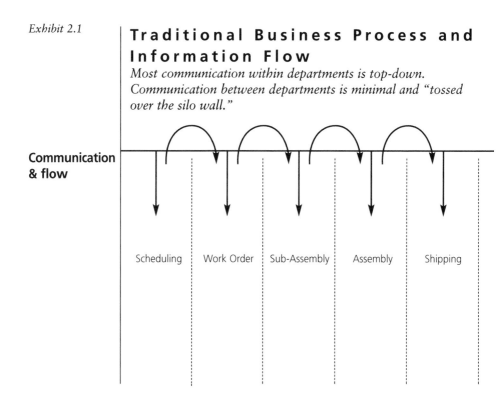

Communication & flow

Scheduling | Work Order | Sub-Assembly | Assembly | Shipping

This structure results in a narrow perspective that does not stimulate process improvement. Finger pointing and blame for mistakes can be quite common. The result is lowered performance and, ultimately, dissatisfied customers. (See Exhibit 2.1: Traditional Business Process and Information Flow.)

Enlightened organizations understand that processes take place horizontally and that information and activities must flow across the organization in a smooth and collaborative way. This system requires working in team formats. People with different areas of expertise work together in a cross-functional team format to ensure that processes and information move across the organization in the most timely, efficient and effective manner. (See Exhibit 2.2: Team-Based Horizontal Organization.)

Exhibit 2.2

Team-Based Horizontal Organization

Communications are horizontal, involving all elements of the process in a cross-functional team format.

Communication & flow follows the process line flow

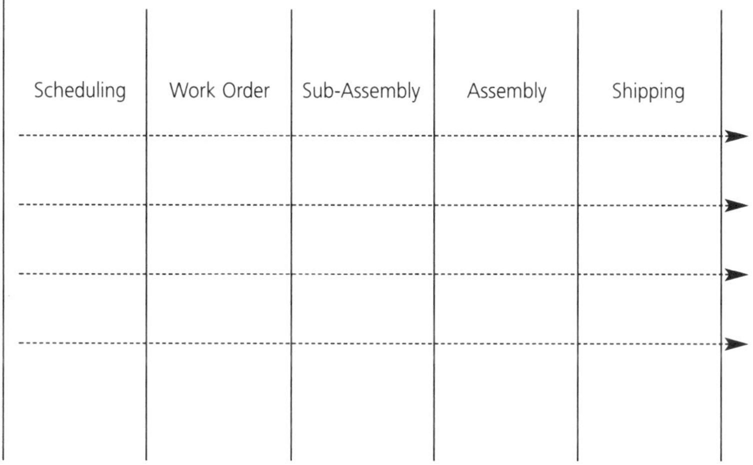

Scheduling	Work Order	Sub-Assembly	Assembly	Shipping

Implementation of the Vision is more effective if the tasks are broken down into bite-sized pieces.

Implementing the Vision is more effective if the tasks are broken down into bite-sized pieces and tackled by teams responsible for developing plans to achieve segments of the Vision. All teams should be given written mandates and timetables to allow them to focus effectively on their specific assignments.

The teams' boundaries and levels of authority should be clearly defined. Some teams are asked to make only recommendations. Others are given authority to implement changes without further approvals, provided the changes are within the parameters of the team's mandate.

Teams invariably need leaders, who set the agenda and act as facilitators in meetings. Like jury forepersons, team leaders should not function as bosses and should generally not have any greater power than other team members. A good team leader knows how to bring out the best in a team by guiding it through the analysis process and by encouraging all team members to share their thoughts and ideas with the group.

Working in a team format is not without its problems and challenges. Sometimes teams have disruptive members with negative attitudes or agendas that are not consistent with those of the rest of the team. When teams do not work well together, it is important for the team leader to guide the team through an open process of understanding the reasons for the problems. Most teams are able to work through the issues and emerge stronger. Disruptive members should be given an opportunity to change their behavior. If that cannot be achieved, the team should vote to remove them.

Our experience has shown that there are some employees and managers who do not work well in a team environment. While not impossible, it is usually hard for these people to function effectively in a TDVBUM environment. It is important to differentiate people who are effective at what they do, but not good at working in teams, from people who are destructive to progress and the team process. The former group can often still be productive, while the latter need to be removed, unless they can change their attitudes and style.

All teams need some ground rules to govern their activities. Although every team should develop and agree on its own set of ground rules consistent with management guidelines, some apply to most teams. One of the most important of these is the commitment to confidentiality. The bonding that arises from sharing thoughts and ideas with teammates is one of the catalysts that spark the creativity that makes teams so effective. Nothing will stifle creativity faster than the fear that something said in a team meeting will be leaked to people outside the team. Consequently, an important ground rule is that nothing discussed within the team is mentioned outside of the team until the team agrees that it is appropriate.

Team leaders should not function like bosses.

Another ground rule is the "no ridicule" principle. One of the most valuable results of team dynamics is the opportunity for brainstorming, a freewheeling and interactive process in which team members work together to generate creative ideas. People who have worked extensively with teams know that some of the best ideas are sparked by other ideas or suggestions that initially seemed inappropriate, off base or even stupid. As a result, the team should welcome all ideas because it will not know until later which ones are truly valuable. (See Part III: Tool 4 for further discussion of brainstorming techniques.)

Teams should also agree on some basic common courtesies. These include regular attendance at meetings, being on time and not speaking while another team member is speaking. With this groundwork in place, teams are ready to contribute the expertise and creativity of all their members as they respond to their mandates.

Bottom-Up Management, appropriately executed in a team format, increases creativity and energy levels within the company significantly. While individuals usually thrive on empowerment, most people are even more stimulated by the camaraderie and interpersonal dynamics that result from working in a team environment.

Types of Teams

Several types of teams can play an important role in a Bottom-Up Management structure.

Project teams are formed with a specific purpose or unique task (example: a team formed to improve productivity in a department). Their life spans could be very short or could extend for months or even years, depending on their tasks, but are unlikely to have a permanent role in the business.

Functional teams are set up to perform specific regular functions in a business and are more permanent in nature than project teams. These could extend from a team working together in a department (example: the accounts receivable team, which works together to manage the accounts receivable function on a continuing basis) to cross-functional teams that focus on a process that crosses many boundaries (example: product development team made up of people from many areas of the business who work together on a permanent, but perhaps part-time, basis to develop new products).

Advisory teams are part of the structure The Parkland Group has developed and used extensively to achieve Bottom-Up Management. These cross-functional and multi-level teams act as a source of ideas and a sounding board for senior management in the development and implementation of the Vision. Advisory teams can be helpful in determining if ideas are sound and will be well received by employees.

Seeking advice and ideas from employees is one of the hallmarks of Bottom-Up Management. Receiving this feedback through the structure of an advisory team can be highly effective. An advisory team can review the ideas and plans developed by other teams (including Vision, drivers of success, and implementation ideas and plans) to ensure that they are likely to work and have taken into account all the issues and nuances of the business that are likely to affect their success. Searching for ways to improve productivity, customer satisfaction and employee motivation are also very valuable and appropriate tasks for advisory teams, which may then recommend creation of project teams.

We have found that advisory teams work even better when management does not handpick the members. If the team members are perceived as management "stooges," the company is unlikely to benefit from the valuable buy-in that can result from this process. For this reason, we recommend giving employees a say in selecting members of the advisory teams.

Seeking advice and ideas from employees is one of the hallmarks of Bottom-Up Management.

Employees can be asked to nominate several people they believe should be on the team. The nominations are tabulated and reviewed by someone independent of senior management[1] to ensure that the team sufficiently represents all functions and levels in the company. Before the teams are finalized, all potential nominees should be interviewed to ensure that they are willing to serve on the team and are likely to make a positive contribution.

Smaller companies might have only one advisory team. Bigger companies and those with multiple locations usually find that it

---

1. The nomination could be reviewed by the human resources department, if trusted by the employees, or by a trained outside facilitator or consultant.

is valuable to have several teams. Advisory teams work best with between eight and twelve members, depending on the size of the company or division. The sizes of project teams can vary from as low as three to as many as ten people. Functional teams can be even larger because they may consist of a whole department.

Teams can have a profound impact on the success of business.[2] The most obvious reason is the value of the ideas and feedback management receives from employees. Another reason is the buy-in generated when employees see that they and their colleagues are valued in developing and reviewing plans. Employees become even more committed to contributing their expertise.

2. Businesses that are parties to collective bargaining agreements should maintain open communication with union officials and leaders and comply with all labor laws before including bargaining unit members on teams. Competent legal counsel should be sought.

Exhibit 2.3

Top-Down Vision and Bottom-Up Management Process

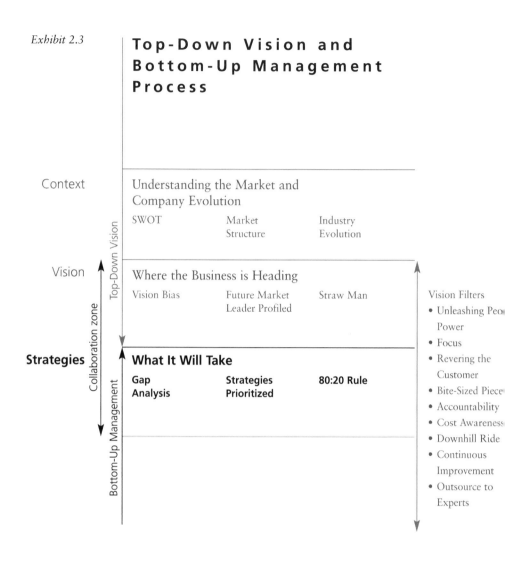

Context	Understanding the Market and Company Evolution		
	SWOT	Market Structure	Industry Evolution

Vision — Where the Business is Heading

	Vision Bias	Future Market Leader Profiled	Straw Man

Strategies — **What It Will Take**

	Gap Analysis	**Strategies Prioritized**	**80:20 Rule**

Top-Down Vision

Bottom-Up Management

Collaboration zone

Vision Filters
• Unleashing People Power
• Focus
• Revering the Customer
• Bite-Sized Pieces
• Accountability
• Cost Awareness
• Downhill Ride
• Continuous Improvement
• Outsource to Experts

Strategies
What will it take to achieve the Vision?

Creating a compelling Vision for the future provides a company with a starting point on its road to success. The gap between the company's current state and future state establishes creative tension. Like a rubber band being stretched, this tension creates energy and sets the stage for the real power of the strategy-development process. Analyzing the gap creates the framework for developing strategies to lead the company to its future state.

Gap Analysis

The objective is to define the strategies on which the company must focus to achieve the Vision. Strategies are the major actions, activities or capabilities that must be put in place to make the Vision a reality. The gap between the current and desired future states provides the basis for development of the strategies needed to achieve the Vision.

The objective is to define the strategies on which the company must focus in order to achieve the Vision.

Identifying the major strategies is a critical step on the road to success, requiring extensive brainstorming and debate. (See Part III: Tool 4, Brainstorming and Analytical Techniques.) A project team selected by the senior leadership team should develop the strategies. The team should be made up of the brightest, most energetic people (from a cross-section of areas throughout the business) who have the ability to think strategically and creatively. The team focuses on developing a comprehensive list of the strategies needed to achieve the company's Vision.

Exhibit 2.4

Strategy Gap

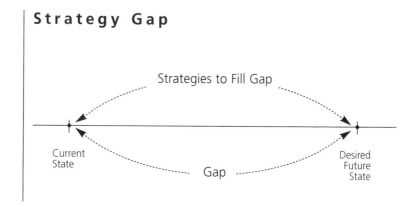

Strategies prioritized

Once the team has developed its list of potential strategies, it should turn its attention to prioritizing the strategies. They should be broken down into the following categories:

- Essential
- Important
- Less important

The strategies needed to achieve the Vision are developed from analyzing the gap between the company's current state and its desired future state.

The team developed to determine the strategies should not focus on how they will be implemented. At this stage, there is a very real danger of being bogged down because of perceived constraints and lack of current capabilities. Instead, the team should be encouraged to focus on the strategies with confidence that the tactics will be dealt with at the next stage.

80:20 Rule

Despite the age-old Judeo-Christian belief that hard work generates success, this is only true if that work is expended on

Exhibit 2.5

Strategy Development
Aspiring Manufacturing Company

Current State	Desired Future State	Strategies to Fill Gap
Poor communications and little teamwork	Collaborative, energized environment	• Involve, inform and empower employees
Cost of poor quality exceeding 20% of sales	Less than 5%	• Understanding, analyzing root causes of quality problems. • Company-wide commitment to eliminate causes
Capable of serving customers in home state	National leader in market share	• Hire and develop rep. network • Develop regional warehousing capability • Develop nationwide brand awareness and desirability
5% Return on Assets	Greater than 20%	• Eliminate finished goods inventory • Outsource non-essential operations

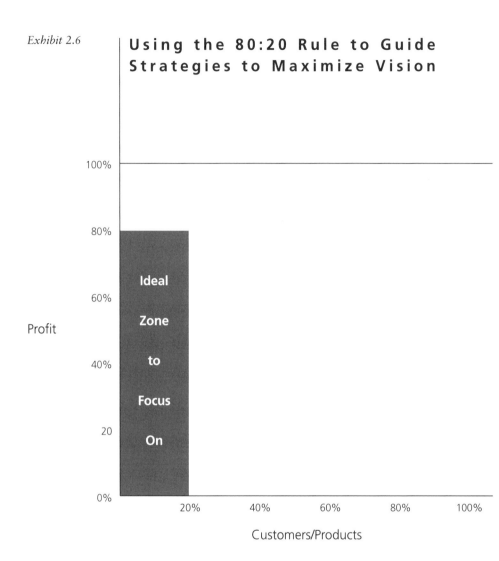

Exhibit 2.6

Using the 80:20 Rule to Guide Strategies to Maximize Vision

Ideal Zone to Focus On

Profit

Customers/Products

activities that contribute to attaining goals. Resources and energy that are not adding value to the Vision are a drain and detract from achieving success. In developing business strategy to achieve the Vision, it is beneficial to steer the company toward those activities and opportunities that add the most value.

The 80:20 rule states that in 80% of businesses—
- 80% of the profit is from 20% of the products and
- 80% of the revenue is from 20% of the customers

While this may seem farfetched, it turns out to be uncannily true in the vast majority of cases. The numbers in particular situations may vary slightly (examples: 75:25, 85:15, etc.), but the general hypothesis is surprisingly reliable.

This fact has very important implications for strategy development. In most circumstances, it will make sense to direct a business toward the twenty percent of products, customers and regions that contribute eighty percent of profits and revenues. This does not mean that the eighty percent that are unprofitable should be abandoned, but it is wise to reconsider the company's approach to them. Strategies may include increasing prices, reducing inventories or reducing costs.

To make these determinations, it is important to utilize activity-based costing, or ABC. (See Part III: Tool 3.) Activity-based costing captures the true cost of producing, delivering and servicing products and customers. It differs significantly from traditional accounting used in generally accepted accounting principles (GAAP) in that it captures all costs and not just manufacturing costs. When ABC is used, it often exposes the lack of profitability of many products, customers and regions. GAAP accounting's shortcomings frequently mask these problems.

An ABC analysis for a Parkland client in the plastic manufacturing business revealed that 80 percent of the invoices gener-

ated losses. These were mostly smaller orders, averaging under $50. Many of these customers were quite demanding, requiring extensive customer service time and attention.

The 80:20 rule can help businesses direct their strategies toward products, customers and markets that will lead to success.

When the costs of the shorter production runs and the customer service were factored into the equation, very few of these orders were profitable. To compound the problem, the company's ability to service its other customers was severely compromised by the time and attention devoted to the unprofitable transactions. The company's strategy was changed to focus on a smaller number of profitable customers. Costs came down and profits increased quickly and significantly.

Using the 80:20 rule, businesses can find many similar opportunities to direct their strategies toward products, customers and markets that will lead to success. A significant amount of expense that is dedicated to unprofitable activities can be eliminated without any adverse impact.

Drivers of Success
What gets measured
gets improved

Countless CEOs have developed Visions for their businesses that have never been achieved. One of the major reasons for this problem is the lack of clear definition of the critical elements for success. Drivers of success are the specific elements of business performance that the company will focus on and measure. They are developed from brainstorming processes that determine the fundamental issues that can truly make the difference between success and failure.

Selected for their ability to help the business achieve its desired Vision, drivers of success are different in every business. Successful businesses know what they are and pursue them vigorously. For example, a Parkland client in the distribution industry concluded that being able to fulfill customers' needs within 24 hours more than 95 percent of the time was essential to its success. As a result, it began to track this driver of success regularly and implemented systems and procedures to ensure continuous improvement of this benchmark.

rivers of success are the things that

e company cares about and focuses

1 continually to put itself in a position

succeed.

Some of the drivers of success are easier to calculate than others. The difficulty in calculating benchmarks does not negate the importance of understanding and being aware of them. Most successful companies are able to develop methods to gauge these items satisfactorily.

Drivers of success can generally be divided into the four elements of the Vision statement:

1. **People/Culture**

    Examples: Turnover rates; safety rates; rates of absen-
    teeism; morale levels; opportunities for training and
    advancement; culture; values; communications

2. **Operations**

    Examples: Utilization rates; productivity; downtime;
    yield/scrap rates; quality; rework; cycle times; asset
    turnover rates; response rates

3. **Customer/Market**

    Examples: Customer satisfaction; value received in rela-
    tion to price paid; complaint rates; defection/attrition
    rates; fill rates; on-time delivery rates; win ratios; mar-
    ket/wallet share; comparable growth rates; average order
    size; backlog; order rates; revenue per unit

4. **Financial**

    Examples: Sales; gross profit margins; variable contribution
    margins; operating profit; net profit; EBITDA (earnings
    before interest, taxes, depreciation and amortization);
    return on assets managed (ROAM); gross margin return
    on inventory (GMROI); inventory turnover rate; accounts
    receivable collection rate (known as day's sales outstanding
    or DSO); earnings per share (EPS); debt/equity rates; return
    on shareholders' equity (ROE); economic value added
    (EVA); break-even point; unit costs; working capital targets

*Paul O'Neill, who was the CEO of Alcoa before he became the
Secretary of the Treasury, used worker safety rates as one of the
most important drivers of success at Alcoa. Jack Welch drove
enormous cost reductions at GE by focusing on Six Sigma, a
process that reduces error rates. Southwest Airlines uses flight
turnaround cycle times as one of its drivers of success.*

Identifying the drivers of success central to achieving a Vision
is critical. Despite a temptation to focus on numerous drivers,

it is important to pick the ones likely to drive success for a particular company. The old adage "what gets measured, gets improved" is very true, but it is important to measure the specific activities that will drive a business to success.

Exhibit 2.7

D r i v e r s   o f   S u c c e s s
Aspiring Manufacturing Company

People/ Culture	Operations	Customers/ Markets	Finance
• Turnover <15% • <5% lost time accidents p.a. • 80% of promotions filled internally • Employee satisfaction rating >80%	• Inventory turnovers >12% • Cost of poor quality <5% • First pass yield >98%	• Fill 98% of orders within 48 hours • 25% market share • Average order size >$5,000	• Sales growth of 20% p.a • >10% operating profit • Cash-to-cash cycle time <100 days • Unit cost <$10

Exhibit 2.8

Vision Statement Components Template

	People/ Culture	Operations	Customers/ Markets	Finance
Vision Summary	*An overview statement summarizing the desired future state of the organization*			
Vision Elements *Where the Business is Heading*	• Skills • Culture • Work Environment	• Cost • Quality • Responsiveness • Innovation	• Markets Served, Products Offered • Customers Targeted • Value Proposition/ Reason to Thrive	• Growth Rates • Profitability Targets • Capital Structure • Return on Investment
Strategy Components *What It Will Take*	• Leadership • People Profile • Layers/Spans of Control • Norms/Values • Accountability	• Processes • Supply Chain Mgmt. Systems • Technology • Infrastructure • Capabilities	• R & D • Mkt. Knowledge • Cust. Knowledge • Channel Dev. • Cust. Satisfaction/ Loyalty • Sales Coverage/ Approach	• Sources/Uses of Capital • Accurate Costing Pricing • Mgmt. Information Forecasting Syst. • Risk/Assessment Mgmt. • Inventory Strategy

Strategy Components
What must be done?

$\mathbf{M}$ost businesses have similar strategy issues or components that must be addressed in developing the plan to fill gaps so that the Vision can be achieved. Exhibit 2.8: Vision Statement Components Template provides examples of the typical strategic components needed to achieve the Vision, including the following:

- The leadership style, people profiles, norms, values and organization structure that will be needed to achieve the company's Vision regarding its culture, work environment and skills needed

- The processes, supply-chain management systems, technology, infrastructure and capabilities that will be needed to achieve the company's Vision and their relationship to cost, quality, responsiveness and innovation

- The research and development, and market and customer knowledge needed to reach the targeted markets and customers with the appropriate products and services

- The development of appropriate sales channels, customer satisfaction strategies and sales coverage to ensure the desired value proposition is achieved, reinforcing the company's "reasons to thrive" (or competitive advantages)

- The sources and uses of capital, costing and pricing strategies, management information and forecasting systems and inventory strategies, as well as the risk assessment and management strategies that will be needed to achieve the desired growth rates, profitability, capital structure and return on investment

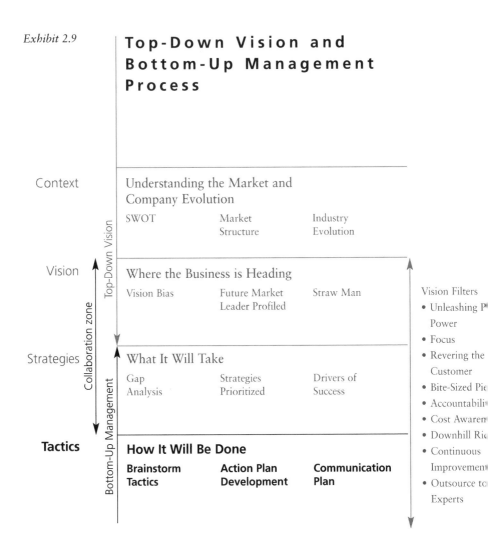

Exhibit 2.9

Top-Down Vision and Bottom-Up Management Process

Context

Understanding the Market and Company Evolution

| SWOT | Market Structure | Industry Evolution |

Vision

Where the Business is Heading

| Vision Bias | Future Market Leader Profiled | Straw Man |

Strategies

What It Will Take

| Gap Analysis | Strategies Prioritized | Drivers of Success |

Tactics

How It Will Be Done

| **Brainstorm Tactics** | **Action Plan Development** | **Communication Plan** |

Top-Down Vision

Bottom-Up Management

Collaboration zone

Vision Filters
- Unleashing P▪ Power
- Focus
- Revering the Customer
- Bite-Sized Pie
- Accountabili▪
- Cost Awaren▪
- Downhill Ri▪
- Continuous Improvemen▪
- Outsource to Experts

Tactics
How it will be done

So far, we have discussed:
- Establishing a context for planning by determining the company's current state and analyzing the market and company evolution
- Developing a Vision for the company's future (its desired future state)
- Developing a set of strategies that will be required to achieve the Vision, after understanding the competitive and internal environments

The next, and pivotal, step is to determine how to execute the strategies. One study of over 2,000 companies suggests that one of the biggest reasons companies fail to create shareholder value is the inability of management to develop and implement growth strategies effectively.[1] Execution is everything. A Vision has little value without a tactical plan that is easy to understand and implement. Success hinges on how well the next step is accomplished: defining how the company will make its Vision a reality.

The tactical plan must be easy to understand and articulate, and everyone in the company must have a role.

Brainstorm Tactics

When the list of strategies has been developed and agreed upon with senior management, the next phase of the Top-Down Vision and Bottom-Up Management process is to develop the

---

1. Chris Zook and James Allen, *The Facts About Growth*, June 1999.

specific tactics to implement the strategies. Cross-functional project teams should be drafted for each major strategy. The teams should be made up of a balanced cross-section of intelligent and knowledgeable people from throughout the company who are respected and have the ability to think creatively. Utilizing the principles of the brainstorming process, each team reviews the Vision and develops a comprehensive list of all the tactics that will be needed to implement its assigned strategy.

For example, consider Happy Homes Furnishings, Inc., a business whose Vision is "To become the leading retailer of home furnishings for middle-class families in the Midwest." A team is asked to develop the tactics for a strategy that encompasses being able to ship 98 percent of its orders within 48 hours.

The tactics that the team might develop to execute this strategy include:
- *Establish three additional distribution centers over the next five years*
- *Develop real-time inventory management and open-to-buy information systems*
- *Set up just-in-time (JIT) supply chains with vendors*
- *Establish SKU management systems to ensure that slow-moving items are discontinued*

Action Plan Development
With the tactics prioritized, the team embarks on a further brainstorming process to develop an action plan for every tactic, focusing attention on the most important tactics first. Each action plan should address:
- A description of the tactic
- The specific steps or action plans that will be needed
- Timelines for completing each step
- Who will be responsible for each step
- Resources that will be needed
- How success will be tracked and measured

Exhibit 2.10

Vision Statement
Action Plan
Happy Homes Furnishing, Inc.

Vision Summary | *To become the leading retailer of home furnishings for middle-class families in the Midwest*

Vision Elements

People/Culture	Operations	Customers/Market	Finance
• Customer-oriented	• Best delivery service in industry	• Affordable but stylish products	• 20% annual growth
• Strong design sense	• Satisfaction guarenteed	• Household income $60,000 to $90,000	• Operating profit of 7% of sales
• Collaborative	• Efficient operations	• Ohio, Indiana, Illinois, Kentucky	• Debt/equity 150%
		• Great value for $	• 15% ROA
		• Free design service	

Strategy A | *Be able to ship 98% of orders within 48 hours*

Tactic 1 | *Establish three additional distribution centers over the next five years to service the planned store growth*

Action Plans

	Owner	Start Date	Due Date	Status	Priority
(i) Conduct a demographic analysis to decide where to locate distribution centers	GM	Jan 10	Apr 15	complete	essential
(ii) Hire real estate brokers to research markets and identify existing buildings or land	SE	Apr 15	June 30	25%	essential
(iii) Conduct own or lease analysis	GM	June 15	July 31	0%	essential
(iv) Retain architects	SE	June 30	July 31	0%	important
(v) Develop financing options	EN	July 31	Sept 30	0%	important
(vi) Contact state and local governments about government assistance	GM	May 1	July 31	0%	important
(vii) Decide on phone systems	MK	Dec 15	Feb 15	0%	less important
(viii) Issue press release	RJ	Feb 15	Feb 28	0%	less important

Exhibit 2.11

Action Plan Details
Happy Homes Furnishing Inc.

Overall Vision	*To become the leading retailer of home furnishings for middle-class families in the Midwest*
Strategy A	*Be able to ship 98% of orders within 48hours*
Action Plan (i)	*Conduct a demographic analysis to decide where to locate distribution centers*

Action Plan Details

	Owner	Start Date	Due Date	Status
Hire marketing firm for complete market assessment	GM	1/1/03	2/15/03	complete
Target areas where future growth fits target markets	LG	2/15/03	3/1/03	25%
Research preliminary real estate environments of target areas	RM	3/2/03	3/10/03	0%
Present top picks to executive team with complete analysis of selection	Team	3/25/03	3/25/03	0%
Consult legal for approved sites	RM	3/26/03	3/31/03	0%
Handoff to real estate team	Team	4/1/03	4/1/03	0%

The action plan should include setting up a system for documentation that is easy to understand. Many teams choose to utilize commercially available project management software. When the team has completed the action plan for its strategy, it should be presented to the senior management team for its review and input. (See Exhibit 2.10: Vision Statement Action Plans and Exhibit 2.11: Action Plan Details.)

When approved by the senior management team, each tactic must be "owned" by a project leader. That leader assembles a project team to supervise and guide the implementation of the action plan. This may or may not be the same team that developed the action plan. As in any management situation, clear parameters with respect to timelines, reporting protocols and measurable results are established and agreed to by both the project team and the senior management team. It is the responsibility of the company's leadership to provide the teams with as much support and direction as necessary to maintain momentum and demonstrate commitment to change.

Throughout the TDVBUM process, it is essential to have excellent communications on a regular basis to explain:
- Why the organization is embarking on the process
- How the process will work
- What it will mean for the company and for individual employees
- Progress made

These communications should come from the CEO, senior leaders and all of the teams that are involved in the process. Communications can take many forms, including:
- Group or "town-hall" meetings
- E-mails
- Newsletters
- Bulletin board postings
- Memorandums

Differentiating Vision, Strategies and Tactics

It can sometimes be difficult to make a clear distinction between Vision, Strategies and Tactics. Exhibit 2.12 sets out descriptions and examples that will help make these important distinctions.

Balancing priorities

One of the significant challenges in embarking on a TDVBUM process is the resulting conflict with people's time and priorities. Most businesses are already stretched thin, even without becoming involved in developing and implementing a Vision. Many people will be asked to serve on one or more teams, and meetings can take considerable time and energy. Colleagues and supervisors may become resentful of people who are absent from their regular duties.

There is often a temptation for businesses to conclude that they are unable to take the time to plan at this level of detail. Our experience has been that these businesses expend vast amounts of energy "fighting fires" and "working harder" rather than working smarter. While the TDVBUM process is time-consuming, virtually every business that has used it has found the time invested infinitely valuable. The clarity that results, the ideas that are developed and the buy-in that is generated justify the time investment many times over.

It is important to be realistic about time commitments. Over-committing out of enthusiasm for the process can backfire. People who feel pressed should be reminded of the value and benefits of the process, but should also reexamine their commitments.

Exhibit 2.12

Vision, Strategies & Tactics
How to differentiate them

	Vision (Where we are going)	Strategies (What it will take)	Tactics (How it will happen)
Examples	Customer-oriented	Hire people who like serving others	Develop psychological evaluation to identify this trait
	Efficient operations	State-of-the-art warehouse design and management systems	Retain warehouse consulting firm with extensive experience & credentials
	Affordable but stylish products	Purchasing personnel to have strong design experience	Rotational training program that includes stints in sales and design depts
	Operating profit of 7% of sales	Gross margins exceeding 50%	Import >25% of products sold

Exhibit 2.13

Vision Statement Components Template

	People/ Culture	Operations	Customers/ Markets	Finance
Vision Summary	*An overview statement summarizing the desired future state of the organization*			
Vision Elements *Where the Business is Heading*	• Skills • Culture • Work Environment	• Cost • Quality • Responsiveness • Innovation	• Markets Served, Products Offered • Customers Targeted • Value Proposition/ Reason to Thrive	• Growth Rates • Profitability Targets • Capital Structure • Return on Investment
Strategy Components *What It Will Take*	• Leadership • People Profile • Layers/Spans of Control • Norms/Values • Accountability	• Processes • Supply Chain Mgmt. Systems • Technology • Infrastructure • Capabilities	• R & D • Mkt. Knowledge • Cust. Knowledge • Channel Dev. • Cust. Satisfaction/ Loyalty • Sales Coverage/ Approach	• Sources/Uses of Capital • Accurate Costing/ Pricing • Mgmt. Information/ Forecasting Systems • Risk/Assessment Mgmt. • Inventory Strategy
Tactics Components *How the Strategies Will Be Implemented*	• Communication • Compensation • Benefits • Staffing/ Recruiting • Training/Dev. • Desired Behaviors	• Software/ Hardware • Policies/ Procedures • Layout/Flow • Measurement Tools • Process Improv.	• Service Levels • Sales & Mktg. Programs (price, place, promotion, product) • Customer Feedback & Analysis	• Internal Controls • Costing/Pricing Systems • Flash Reports • Cash Management • Working Capital Management • Manage ROA by division, department, product line, SKU

Tactics Components
Boiling it down to the critical steps

Successfully implementing the desired Vision and related strategies requires addressing a broad range of tactics, which usually include the following:

- Communication, compensation, benefits, staffing, recruiting, training systems and development needs to achieve desired culture, skills and organizational effectiveness
- The necessary software/hardware, policies and procedures, layout and flow, measurement tools and process improvements to achieve desired operational processes, supply chain, technology, infrastructure and capabilities
- Service levels, sales and marketing programs, customer feedback and analysis systems, and market research needed to achieve desired customer, product and market knowledge and customer satisfaction targets
- The internal controls, costing/pricing systems, flash reports, cash and working capital management systems, and regular and accurate tracking of return on assets managed (ROAM) by division, department, product line and SKU

Part III

Bottom-Up Management Tools

*"Give a man a fish and
you feed him for a day.*

*Teach him how to fish and
you feed him for a lifetime."*

Lao Tzu
Chinese Philosopher

Bottom-Up Management: Tool 1

Lean

Lean, But Not Mean
Less is more

For Top-Down Vision and Bottom-Up Management to be successful, employees must have the tools to be effective. One of the best is commonly referred to as "Lean"[1] thinking. Lean thinking is essentially the speeding up of processes throughout a business by eliminating waste and inefficiency. The objective: significantly reduced total processing or cycle time.

Lean is a way of operating a business that offers tremendous benefits if appropriately implemented. Its principles and practice are well known by most large publicly traded businesses. However, below the Fortune 500 only a small percentage of businesses are familiar with the term Lean. Even fewer understand it or successfully implement it.

Lean thinking is the speeding up of processes throughout a business by eliminating waste and inefficiency.

The benefits of Lean can be so significant that we believe its principles played a very meaningful role in the impressive profit improvement large companies enjoyed in the last decade of the 20th century. There was a rise in profit for the Fortune 500 from $93.3 billion in 1990 to $444 billion in 2000, an increase of 376 percent.

1. The term Lean was coined by a group of engineers who spent 1985 to 1991 in the field comparing many automotive manufacturers. At the end of their mission they concluded that The Toyota Production System was the most "Lean" of all auto manufacturers.

When the Lean method is adopted by an organization and taught to all management and employees, it becomes the one of the cornerstones of TDVBUM. Lean principles guide the Vision when all teams are trained to use the Lean approach to develop Bottom-Up improvement plans.

The creative problem solving needed to identify and eliminate waste cannot be generated with command-and-control management.

While much of the Lean methodology is applied in the manufacturing environment, it is just as applicable and valuable in non-manufacturing activities. Service businesses ranging from distribution to engineering services or fast food can benefit tremendously from this approach. Back-room operations like accounting, product development, estimating and customer service can achieve enormous gains in productivity by applying Lean thinking.

Lean incorporates many different disciplines to achieve its superior performance. Some of the building blocks of Lean systems are:

- **JIT (Just-in-time)** – Producing just what is needed, when it is needed, in the amount needed, with the minimum materials, equipment, labor and space.
- **5-S** – An organized and systematic approach to housekeeping and workplace organization to improve efficiency and drive out waste.
- **Kanban** – Simple visual signals to initiate action or activity to facilitate a JIT mode. In a manufacturing environment, this could be an instruction to an upstream department to supply a component needed to complete a product to satisfy a customer demand. In an engineering firm, it might be an instruction to commence detailed drawings after client's approval of the conceptual drawings.
- **Continuous Flow** – (Also known as one-piece flow or single-piece flow) Processing methods that group different

functional areas of expertise required for a specific process into the same area, enabling products or paperwork to move more rapidly through the process. The goal is to reduce or eliminate the wasted time that results from waiting caused by batching work in specialized functional areas. The ultimate goal is to achieve a flow of one piece at a time between operations. This approach can reduce cycle times[2] and enhance productivity and quality.

Consider the typical process for designing and quoting a new job. In most businesses, all of the functional specialties are segregated and may even be in different locations or cities. Each specialty completes a series of tasks before passing the work to the next. The process might start in the sales department, which would write up the inquiry. A batch of inquiries is delivered to the design department periodically, perhaps daily, every few days or weekly. When design has finished its work, the batch is delivered to the estimating department, which prices the job. The estimate sheet is then sent back to sales to present the proposal to the customer. This process could take days, weeks or even months. The paperwork often sits in someone's in tray for an inordinate length of time before any action is taken.

In a Lean, continuous-flow environment, all of the people in the process work in a team format, usually in close proximity to each other. Instead of the slow, sequential batch process, the functional disciplines work together to move the quote through the process very quickly. Design is aware of the prospects sales are working on and is offering input early in the process to improve the design and lower the cost. Estimating is giving input to design to help them create a more cost-effective design. All of the people in the

---

2.   Cycle time is the elapsed time from the first step in a process to the time the process is complete.

While much of the Lean methodology is applied in the manufacturing environment, it is just as applicable and valuable in non-manufacturing activities.

process are focused on achieving the ultimate goal of satisfying the customer. The result is invariably a better product, at a lower cost, and a happier customer.

- **Quick Changeovers/ SMED (Single-Minute Exchange of Dies)** – A systematic approach to reduce setup times from one product to another with the goal of reducing the time of setups to a single digit and even eventually eliminating setups. In a manufacturing environment, time-consuming setups and changeovers reduce production efficiency significantly and can contribute to a lack of flexibility. A fundamental goal of Lean is to make setup and changeover times so brief that they facilitate a high degree of production flexibility, allowing JIT to be a practical reality.

The objective of Lean is to identify the value stream[3] and eliminate the "rocks" that slow progress and extend cycle times. The ultimate ambition is to significantly reduce the time it takes for the company to respond to a customer's needs. Lean is based on the belief that the faster a process successfully moves through the system, the less waste and inefficiency there will be and the lower the cost.[4]

3. The value stream is the symbolic river of value-added activities that are necessary to produce a product or deliver a service, from conception to customer. Activities that are not value-added are symbolic diversions of the river's most efficient flow, extending process times and contributing to poor quality.

4. GE Corporation implemented its own version of Lean that it refers to as Six Sigma. (Lean focuses on standardization and cycle time reduction, while Six Sigma attacks the variation from the standard.) Essentially a focus on reducing error rates, Six Sigma has contributed significantly to GE's improved profits. GE learned the techniques of Six Sigma from Motorola.

Most organizations are quite oblivious to extensive waste and inefficiency. They have become accustomed to it and have not been trained to identify its symptoms or causes. Many activities that companies believe are essential are the biggest culprits. When leaders and employees are trained to identify waste and inefficiency, they are often shocked because the amount of waste far exceeds the level they anticipated. This realization creates an opportunity for the business to improve.

Properly implementing Lean requires a culture based on teamwork. The creativity that is needed to identify and eliminate waste cannot be generated with command-and-control management. The interdependent and collaborative interaction of TDVBUM is far more conducive to generating the ideas needed to become Lean.

Exhibit 3.1.1

Seven Buckets of Waste: Non-Value-Added Activities

Over-production: producing more inventory than is needed to respond to customers' immediate needs, wasting human, capacity and financial resources

Inventory: inventory above the minimum levels required to manage flow and maintain throughput

Waiting: time spent waiting for work instructions or work from upstream operations. Can also take the form of parts waiting for further processing

Transportation: unnecessary movement of people, equipment, materials or paperwork resulting from inefficient layouts or process design

Motion: movement that does not add value to product

Waste in the work itself: the process or cycle is complicated with excessive steps or time, including duplication of effort

Defects: defective products, scrap and reworked production

Becoming Lean
Working smarter

The first step in the Lean journey is to identify and map out the value stream. In order to do this, it is important to understand the meaning of value-added activities (VAs) and non-value-added activities (NVAs). VAs are those actions that transform or shape raw material, information or services to meet internal or external customers' needs. NVAs (also referred to as "Muda," the Japanese term for waste) are actions that consume time, resources or space, but do not add to the value of a product or service.

Understanding these key terms makes it possible to map out the current value stream from supplier to customer. Once this has been accomplished, it is time to create a game plan to attack the major areas of non-value-added activities and develop a map of how that process will work in the future.

Non-value-added activities are actions that consume time, resources or space, but do not add to the value of a product or service.

In most processes that have not been subjected to a Lean discipline, the NVAs far outnumber the VAs. In fact, The Parkland Group has analyzed many processes where VAs represented less than 20 percent of the total activities. Every NVA step in a process adds time and cost, reducing competitiveness and profitability. The scale of the opportunity for improvement is the main reason that Lean can be so valuable.

All businesses can improve productivity by using Bottom-Up

Management (see Kaizen teams in Part III, Tool 2) to analyze processes, identify NVAs and suggest solutions. Most NVAs will belong in one of the seven buckets of waste reflected in Exhibit 3.1.1.

Successful companies commit to continuous improvement by the relentless pursuit of productivity.[1] The implementation of Lean principles throughout a company is without doubt one of the best ways to accomplish continuous improvement. All significant processes should be examined regularly to identify NVAs and eliminate them.

In most processes that have not been subjected to a Lean discipline, the non-value-added activities far outnumber the value-added ones.

---

1. Relentlessly pursuing productivity is the third foundation of a turbocharged company, described in *The Turbocharged Company*, Goddard and Brown, York, 1995.

Lean Principles
Focusing on customer demand

The essence of a Lean environment is continuous flow in a just-in-time format with pull-through scheduling. Processes are executed in a substantially continuous motion with minimal interruptions, stoppages or wasted actions. A vital hallmark of Lean is making-to-order instead of building speculative inventory. Production processes do not begin until the customer gives the signal, represented by a purchase order. As a result, production information flows through the organization in a pull-through format, with all actions and energy focused on known customer demand.

For continuous flow, the workflow is arranged so that the travel distance between activities is minimal. This is commonly known as cellular processing, where all activities in the process are arranged in close proximity, resembling a cell. In addition, when an activity is completed, the product is immediately passed on to the next activity rather than waiting for a pile to be completed and moved. In essence, in a Lean environment items are moving through the process in batches of one. This method facilitates markedly greater process speed, generating the valuable benefits of Lean.

Continuous flow generally necessitates greater teamwork. Rather than working as somewhat independent specialists, people work in a collaborative manner, maintaining desired process speed by helping teammates if they run into problems. Worker cross training and flexibility are important. Good employees who are able to perform multiple tasks become even more valuable and respected.

Most business processes move in a batch format rather than continuous flow, with materials or paperwork moving slowly through a business from department to department in batches or piles. The operation is laid out based on functional specialties. All similar functions (example: punch presses, engineers) are located in the same area. (See Exhibit 3.1.2: Batch Manufacturing for a typical layout of a plant setup in a batch mode.)

In most batch processes, as much as 90 percent of the total cycle time is waiting time.

The main reason that batch processing is slow is that materials or paperwork are often stacked in a pile before and after the process, with no work being done on them. In most batch processes, as much as 90 percent of the total cycle time is waiting time. (Examples: requests for quotes waiting in the estimators' in-trays; work-in-process waiting to be checked by an inspector before moving to the next station; sheet metal blanks waiting to be stamped.) Waiting time is one of the most prevalent non-value-added activities, and one that offers the some of the best opportunities for Lean improvement.

Non-value-added activities go unnoticed in many batch environments. People are often so busy fighting the daily fires (which are primarily NVAs) that they do not recognize the inefficiency surrounding them. Because a process in a batch environment is expected to take a long time, it is sometimes barely noticeable that certain activities make it even slower. Inefficiency becomes an accepted part of the standard operating practice.

Another problem with batch processing is cumbersome and unreliable scheduling. When an order comes in, most companies in a batch environment quote delivery times of several weeks or even months to give their system time to direct the paperwork and materials through the process.

Exhibit 3.1.2

Typical Batch Manufacturing Chart

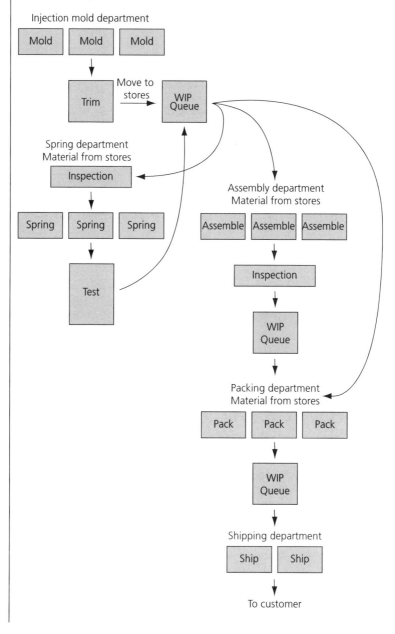

Exhibit 3.1.3

Typical Continuous Flow or Cellular Manufacturing Layout

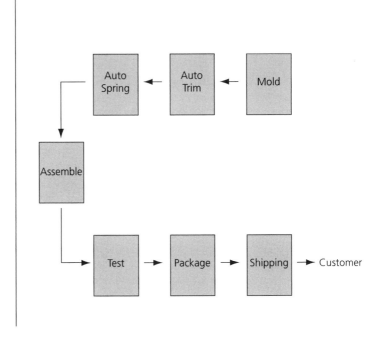

To compensate for long delivery times, most batch manufacturers try to predict what customers will order and then build inventory to satisfy the anticipated orders. Unfortunately, customers are not as predictable as companies hope and the inventory is seldom exactly what customers want. Many businesses respond to this by building even more inventory, determined to get it right. They clog up their capacity, making inventory that might never be sold. Ironically, the building of inventory often renders them unable to respond quickly to actual customer demand.

Lean operations are typically set up with the equipment and functional expertise needed for the process in close proximity

Exhibit 3.1.4

Comparison of Lean Conversion

Before	Total Steps	16
	Value-Added Steps	5
	Non-Value-Added Steps	11
	% Value-Added Steps	31%
	Speed of Thru-put	3 weeks
After	Total Steps	7
	Value-Added Steps	5
	Non-Value-Added Steps	2
	% Value-Added Steps	71%
	Speed of Thru-put	43 seconds
	Improvement of Cycle Time	99.9%

Paperwork or process is moved quickly through the system in a continuous flow with minimal queuing between activities. (See Exhibit 3.1.3: Continuous/Cellular Flow Manufacturing for an example of a plant set up in a Lean format. Also see Exhibit 3.1.4: Comparison of Lean Conversion, for an analysis of the improvements resulting from the lean conversion.)

Lean's goal is to shorten the process cycle time so measurably that finished goods inventory is virtually unnecessary for manufacturers. Companies become able to wait until they have received an order from a customer before beginning the production process.

> *A vital hallmark of Lean is making-to-order instead of building speculative inventory.*

Dell Computer Corporation is a shining example. Their finished goods inventory consists primarily of peripheral products, such as hard drive and printers. They produce computers only when order are received and in many cases, they are able to deliver within a few days, unlike many of their competitors, who often take weeks.

In a Lean environment, where speed of processes is paramount, NVAs have no place to hide. People throughout the company are trained to recognize them and know that they contribute to inefficiency and increased cost. Like accidents at the side of a freeway that cause traffic to slow down to a crawl, NVAs become very noticeable in a Lean environment. People examine them to find the root causes and develop corrective actions to eliminate them permanently. The constant attack on NVAs inspired by a Lean approach always results in major productivity gains.

Setting Up
for Success
The pit-stop approach

To achieve continuous flow in a manufacturing environment, it is essential to reduce setup and changeover times significantly. Whenever the concept of continuous flow is introduced to managers, however, their initial reaction is invariably the same: "That will never work at our company because it takes too long to change over our machines. We are far better off making our products in big batches so that we can generate manufacturing efficiencies." The obstacles are incorrectly perceived as insurmountable.

Dramatic reductions in setup and changeover times are easily attainable and essential for creating the production flexibility needed to operate productively in a Lean format.

Businesses that have historically operated in a batch mode have generally paid little attention to reducing setup and changeover times. These companies tend to operate with long production runs before a changeover is required. They usually view setup and changeover times as insignificant compared to the production run time, even though these changeover times often take hours to accomplish. This results in lengthy cycle times, high inventories and excessive non-value-added activities.

When proponents of Lean began to convince managers that long production runs were not as efficient as they believed, they started to pay more attention to reducing setup and changeover times. Companies that realize that batch manu-

Exhibit 3.1.5

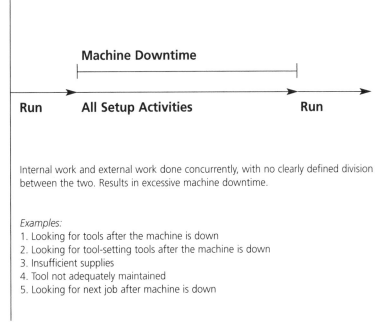

Stage 1
Intermingled Setup Reduction

Machine Downtime

Run   **All Setup Activities**   **Run**

Internal work and external work done concurrently, with no clearly defined division between the two. Results in excessive machine downtime.

Examples:
1. Looking for tools after the machine is down
2. Looking for tool-setting tools after the machine is down
3. Insufficient supplies
4. Tool not adequately maintained
5. Looking for next job after machine is down

facturing is an outmoded approach are now scrambling to speed up processes by reducing changeover times.

Achieving significant reductions in set-up and changeover times is achieved in the same manner as all other productivity enhancements in a Lean environment. First, there is analysis o the process, then the identification of non-value-added activi ties and finally a plan of action to reduce or eliminate NVAs

Any process can be separated into VA and NVA activities; setup and changeovers are no exception. In addition, a changeover process can be divided even further into two additional types o activities, internal and external. Internal activities are define as changeover work that can be performed only when the machine is "down" (inoperative). External, on the other hand

Exhibit 3.1.6

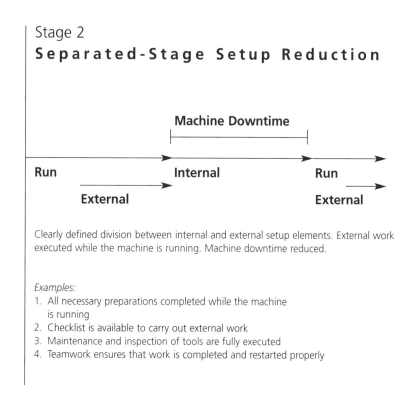

Stage 2
Separated-Stage Setup Reduction

Clearly defined division between internal and external setup elements. External work executed while the machine is running. Machine downtime reduced.

Examples:
1. All necessary preparations completed while the machine is running
2. Checklist is available to carry out external work
3. Maintenance and inspection of tools are fully executed
4. Teamwork ensures that work is completed and restarted properly

is changeover work that can be done while the machine is in operation. This can include activities that can be grouped into gathering, positioning, sorting, adjusting or just pure waste.

Changing the timing of the activities associated with setups can make important progress toward setup reduction. The key objective is to identify external activities being performed while a machine is down and, instead, perform them while the machine is running. This simple practice will considerably reduce the amount of time the machine is inoperative. (See Exhibits 3.1.5 to 3.1.8, which show the four stages of improving setup reduction.)

The best way to reduce setup times is to analyze each step of the changeover from start to finish. Each step is recorded and described on a setup observation form. (See Appendix 2.) The

Exhibit 3.1.7

Stage 3
Converted Work Setup Reduction

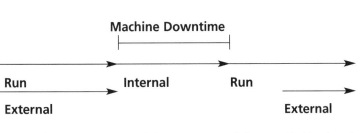

Focus shifts to converting internal elements to external elements. Machine downtime reduced further.

Examples:
1. Standardizing tools
2. Removing adjustments from startup
3. Bolt sizes standardized (with minimum # or no threads)
4. Support equipment and fixtures standardized

description should include the time required for each step and whether it is internal. The step should then be further dissected and labeled as exchanging, gathering, positioning, adjusting, or NVA.

Videotaping a changeover is an excellent analysis tool. The camera is focused only on the area of the machine involved in the changeover. Taping begins the moment the machine is down because of changeover. The camera runs until the machine is up and producing good parts. (This includes first-piece approval.)

After the changeover is complete, the setup reduction team (operators, supervisor, maintenance, etc.) should review the tape. The video invariably astonishes even the most efficient setup personnel. The frequency of employees moving in and

Exhibit 3.1.8

Stage 4
Advanced-Stage Setup Reduction

Machine Downtime

Run →   **Internal**   **Run**

External   **External**

Continuing efforts are focused toward elimination of internal work and shorting the external work through more innovative means. Approaching SMED (single-minute-exchange dies).

Examples:
1. Convert bolts to hydraulic fasteners
2. Setup made into a "kit" form
3. Tools, molds, and fixtures standardized
4. Heights and widths standardized to simplify fastening and adjustments (with their possible elimination)
5. Performance is charted, graphing trends

out of the picture and the time no work is being performed on the machine surprise them. These are signals of the external activities that need to be addressed.

The team should also consider everyday examples of setup that are accomplished with most of the external activities removed. The pit crew in car racing is an excellent example and can provide a good model for the team. A pit crew cannot afford to include external activities during a pit stop, such as looking for a wrench or car jack. It would guarantee defeat. With this image in mind, the setup reduction team can begin to recommend and implement some changes to its process.

Internal activities also offer many scenarios for improvement. For example, in every setup reduction, bolts should be viewed as the enemy. Screwing and unscrewing bolts are non-value-added activities. The first step is to make all bolts the same size. This not only eliminates the need for multiple wrenches, but also reduces time spent locating the correct tool. During a Kaizen event at a client of Parkland's, we actually welded a wrench to a bolt, eliminating time looking for tools. In addition, reducing the number of threads to get the proper amount of clamping power needed may greatly reduce time spent screwing and unscrewing. Ideally, the goal should be to eliminate all bolts, perhaps with quick-disconnect fasteners.[1]

Businesses that have historically operated in a batch mode have generally paid little attention to reducing setup and changeover times.

In addition to making internal activities more efficient, the setup team should consider changing internal activities to external ones. To convert internal to external, it is worthwhile to consider ideas such as preheating molds and doing end-of-run reports to eliminate poor die conditions. When the mindset for change is in place, Bottom-Up Management teams will prove that opportunities for improvement abound.

The SMED concept sets a goal to achieve "Single Minute Exchange of Dies." While this is often an ambitious goal, most businesses can achieve significant reductions in changeover times. Reductions from several hours to less than thirty minutes are not uncommon. Dramatic reductions in setup and changeover times are easily attainable and essential for creating the production flexibility needed to operate productively in a Lean format.

1.　Engineers should be consulted to determine that changes do not compromise safety.

Error Proofing
Making it easier to compete

To achieve Lean (the speeding up of business processes), it is essential to eliminate or substantially reduce the number of defects in any given business system. If this is not accomplished, process time will inevitably stretch.

There is a never-ending cycle with defects. When quality is suspect, production will exceed actual customer requirements in an attempt to meet delivery dates. When production is making more products than required by the first customer, a second customer's order waits to be filled. When the second customer waits, the third order gets even lower priority, and so on. Progression is geometric. The more orders, the more machine time is required. The result: More equipment and space are needed. All these problems are created by compensating for defective products.

Machine time and space are only part of the story for defects. Massive amounts of resources are required to battle quality issues, such as tracking systems and inspectors. A "hidden factory" exists in every company that employs batch-manufacturing techniques. The hidden factory is the behind-the-scene process of sorting, finding, correcting and documenting defective products. The laborious inspection functions can add as much as twenty percent to operating costs. Companies that continue to use batch-operation tactics are finding it increasing difficult to compete.

Error proofing, pioneered by Shigeo Shingo (an industrial engineer at Toyota), is the preferred method to battle defects.

Error proofing, often called poka-yoke (pronounced POH-kah Yoh-kay), prevents a defect from occurring, whereas inspection captures the error after the fact. Error proofing relies on trained operators to prevent defects by employing simple tools and fixtures where possible.

A few examples of error proofing:
- Activation buttons on press machines that require both buttons to be depressed at the same time before the machine is activated, preventing operators from putting their hands in the press during operation
- Jigs that allow a part to be put in only one way, the correct way, before an operation can proceed
- Connection devices that can connect only one way
- Computer controls that deny access to a non-conforming process

One of the biggest benefits of error proofing is the shortened feedback loop of defect information. Operators who catch their own errors are likely to develop cures that attack the root cause of the problem during the production run. This quick response is instrumental in attaining superior quality standards. Incorporating error proofing into the manufacturing system will enable business processes to become Lean, building to customer orders.

Inspection, on the other hand, is inaccurate and time-consuming. It relies on quality-trained employees whose sole job is to find errors and suggest corrective action, sometimes months after the defective product was manufactured. One of the biggest problems with inspection is the variation of the inspection process itself. Each person inspecting might have a different perspective on quality standards, leading to variation. Consider this test: Ask five different people to count how many times the letter "f" appears in the paragraph below.

A farmer found that his field of alfalfa had a certain type of fungus on it. The fungus was part of a family of parasitic microbes. The only answer that the farmer had found to fight the feisty fungus was to spray his fields with a toxic chemical that was not certified. It was the only method that offered him any hope of success. Unfortunately, when the farmer began to spray his fields, the FDA agent was in the area. The federal agent's opinion of the fungus was that it was not at a stage of significant concern. He offered the farmer a choice: Stop the contamination of the flora of the region or face a substantial fine. The farmer halted the spraying of his alfalfa fields.

Error-proofing processes take the guess-work out of quality control.

It is likely that the five people who count will come up with five different answers. (The correct answer can be found at the end of the Glossary at the conclusion of this book.) This is a glaring example of the failures of inspection. Error-proofing processes take the guessing game out of quality control. Foolproof devices ensure that products are sound and quality is consistent, making it easier to compete successfully.

Going with the Flow
Removing the rocks in the value stream

All products or services are brought to market through some type of process. Businesses transform material or knowledge into a form for which a customer is willing to trade. Lean manufacturing refers to these series of activities as "the value stream." The value stream encompasses all activities required to make transformation a reality.

There are two types of value streams:
1. Total value stream – starting at molecules that create the raw materials all the way to the end users
2. Plant value stream – from the receiving dock to shipping within a particular factory (plant)

The beginning point for Lean transformation is a value stream map (VSM). This is a diagrammatic representation of the product or process journey throughout the value stream. The following information is required to map the value stream:
1. Value-added time
2. Non-value-added time
3. Inventory buildup
4. Information required to trigger actions associated with the product family
5. The supplier
6. The customer
7. Customer requirements
8. Cycle times
9. Number of operators required
10. Up-time %
11. Changeover times

The process starts by examining all products or services and grouping them in similar routings (product families). A high-level product family should be selected, and its current state should be mapped.

Value stream mapping activities should commence at the end of the process closest to the customer. This could be shipping or a natural process break such as a paint line. Starting at the end provides a clear picture of the customer links, helping set the pace for upstream and other feeding operations.

The beginning point for Lean transformation is a value stream map (VSM).

Roofs R Us, Inc. was having difficulty meeting customer requirements. Senior management and the owners decided to take the Lean plunge. They began their journey with a high-level value stream map to highlight high-impact areas.

The company was running batches in lots of 20,000. They frequently shipped incomplete orders to their biggest customer, Acme Corp. Overtime and quality problems were very high. The company was carrying large amounts of inventory to cover the operational difficulties.

Each operation on the floor was scheduled individually. Raw material was delivered weekly based on a monthly purchase order the company supplied to its main vendor, Steel Co. The company also delivered weekly to Acme Corp. Acme sent its requirements daily to production control. Exhibit 3.1.9 reflects the value stream map for Roofs R Us before any changes were made to the process.

The next step is to configure a "future state map" of the value stream (See Exhibit 3.1.10). This is achieved by redesigning the process to compress cycle times dramatically by the reduction

Exhibit 3.1.9

Value Stream Mapping

Current State Map

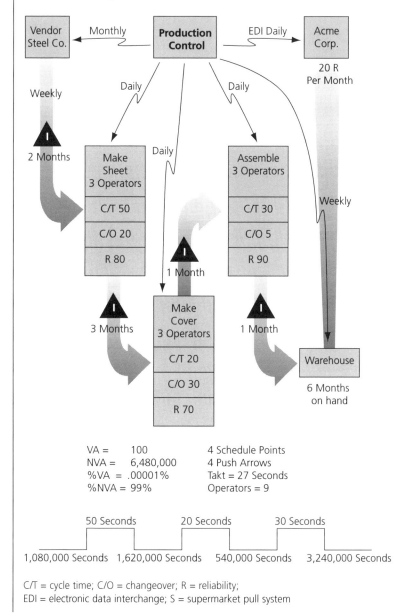

VA = 100 4 Schedule Points
NVA = 6,480,000 4 Push Arrows
%VA = .00001% Takt = 27 Seconds
%NVA = 99% Operators = 9

50 Seconds 20 Seconds 30 Seconds

1,080,000 Seconds 1,620,000 Seconds 540,000 Seconds 3,240,000 Seconds

C/T = cycle time; C/O = changeover; R = reliability;
EDI = electronic data interchange; S = supermarket pull system

Exhibit 3.1.10

Value Stream Mapping

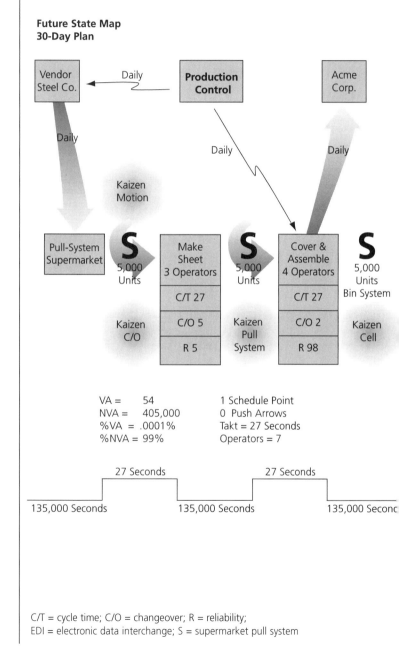

Future State Map
30-Day Plan

VA =   54   1 Schedule Point
NVA =   405,000   0 Push Arrows
%VA = .0001%   Takt = 27 Seconds
%NVA = 99%   Operators = 7

C/T = cycle time; C/O = changeover; R = reliability;
EDI = electronic data interchange; S = supermarket pull system

of the NVA steps. Incorporating pull-through scheduling into the value stream facilitates the reduction of the cycle time.

The first change Roofs R Us made was related to its raw material vendor. Roofs R Us began a two-bin system and instituted a daily "milk run" with Steel Co. Each day the vendor began to replenish the materials used by the company the previous day. This was augmented by a monthly plan of demand from Roofs R Us.

Next, a Kaizen (see Part III: Tool 2) event combined the cover and assembly operations, and successfully reduced the Takt time of this operation to 27 seconds by eliminating excess travel and motion. These changes enabled Roofs R US to establish one scheduling point (assembly) and create flow upstream. Kaizen events were also held to implement a bin system for finished goods and a 'supermarket' between the sheet and assembly operations. Exhibit 3.1.10 sets out the revised value stream map for this operation.

A gap analysis should be performed after the future state map has been completed. The gap analysis will be the guide to future Kaizen events and processing changes to achieve the future state. Implementation plans should be kept in timing windows of sixty to ninety days. This approach forces quick change and will help keep the employees motivated and focused.

Achieving and maintaining the future state can be facilitated by a value stream leader, a person who has responsibility for managing the complete value stream. This approach is a deviation from typical management philosophy. In the past, the leaders, supervisors, foreman or managers never had responsibilities for an entire process and in some cases were oblivious to upstream or downstream activities. The impact of a value stream leader can be dramatic.

A key in the Lean conversion is to make the process transparent. Using VSM will highlight the areas that are the biggest barriers to the desired future state. VSM is a never-ending cycle of current state and future state (continuous-improvement cycle). Generally the value-added activities in the value stream account for less than one percent of the total time; ten percent is considered an outstanding level. Even world-class organizations have plenty of opportunity to reduce waste.

Exhibit 3.1.11

Takt Time Calculation

A	Number of shifts a day	**3**
B	Shifts x length of shift = total available hours (A x 8)	**24**
C	Total hours minus breaks, lunch, pre-work meetings = available production time (B - 3 hours)	**21**
D	Total available production time x 60 = minutes available (C x 60)	**1,260**
E	Total minutes available x 60 = seconds available (D x 60)	**75,600**
F	Units required per month	**20,000**
G	Number of days in month	**21**
H	Units required per production day (F/G)	**952.381**
I	Seconds per day/units required per day (E/H) = seconds per unit	**79.38**

Takt = 79.38 seconds per unit per shift

Takt Time
Synchronization of activities

A steady stream of production that is balanced with customer demand is essential for continuous-flow production in a Lean environment. Accurately measuring and monitoring "takt" times can achieve this goal.

Takt is a German word that means musical meter or "beat of the drum." The Toyota Production System employs takt to describe the rate of customer demand or the rate the customer is buying a given product or service. Knowing takt time (see Exhibit 3.1.11) is critical to eliminating the waste from all business systems. Processes not synchronized with takt time will result in overproduction or underproduction. Excess inventory and late shipments are both undesirable states. Takt time is determined by:

Takt times are the cornerstone of Lean implementation.

- Calculating the amount of available production time per shift (A)
- Knowing the rate of customer demand per shift (B)
- Dividing available production (A) by rate of customer demand (B) to find takt time.

The idea is to identify all tributaries that feed a particular value stream. Then determine the rate at which a product is required to feed downstream demand. Next, synchronize the processes using takt time as the pacemaker in each process to link them. Takt time helps make the process clearly visible and sets the rate of production for the entire value stream.

Once the analysis is complete, companies may find that processes have too much capacity or not enough. Businesses that measure performance based on utilization may need to adjust their thinking and costing methods, in order to justify idling production. Businesses that find themselves in bottleneck situations (not able to meet demand) need to ask these questions:

1. How long are the setups?
2. What is the uptime percentage?
3. Do operators work through breaks and lunches?
4. Is the equipment cycling at standard rates?
5. Can any other equipment be modified to increase capacity?
6. Can a Kanban be used to stimulate flow?

Processes not synchronized with takt time will result in overproduction or underproduction.

Ninety-nine percent of the bottleneck issues will be addressed by analyzing these problems. Takt is also very helpful in determining the staffing of a given product family. The first step is to determine the cycle time using real-time shop floor observations (excluding wasted activities that can be eliminated). Once this is determined, divide the cycle time by the takt time. The result will be the ideal staffing for the process in question.

Takt times are the cornerstone of Lean implementation. Takt is essential to achieving a truly Lean environment, producing just enough product at just the right time to eliminate excess inventories and variable costs in the system. Exhibit 3.1.12 reflects an example of ideal loading of production that is coordinated with customer demand.

Takt time management can be equally important in non-manufacturing environments. Consider an airline check-in counter: Determining the takt time will help determine the number of ticket agents, baggage handlers and security personnel required.

Exhibit 3.1.12

The Ideal Loading

Standard Operations:
In Sync with Customer Demand

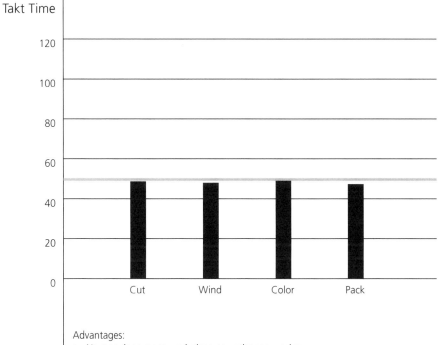

Takt Time

Advantages:
- No one does more work than any other co-worker
- No bottlenecks in the cell – smooth flow
- Each operator adds the same amount of value to the product
- Reduced inventory
- No batching

Benefits of Lean
No place for waste to hide

Speed kills on the highway, but it can be a lifesaver in a business environment. By focusing on cycle times, businesses can dramatically reduce waste, inefficiency and customer response time, presenting opportunities for a host of additional benefits.

To reduce cycle time, the starting point is to identify and analyze non-value-added activities; the next step is to develop and implement plans to reduce or eliminate them. This is best done utilizing another Bottom-Up Management tool known as Kaizen, discussed in the next section. If this is successfully accomplished, the business will generally enjoy many benefits, some of which are discussed below.

Lean processes can be a company's best sales tool.

Operating costs will decline noticeably when NVAs are reduced. For example, if the travel distance between operations is reduced or eliminated, the company will need fewer forklifts, and their related operating costs will be reduced. If a business is able to modify its production procedures so that its scrap and rework rates are reduced, labor and material costs will be reduced. By reducing process cycle times, a business is able to improve its customer response time. Responsiveness can become a major competitive advantage because it allows both the company and its customers greater flexibility.

In a Lean environment, there is a reduction in capital invested. With less inventory, companies usually discover they have more floor space and warehouses than they need. The increased efficiency that comes from Lean and the elimination of excess inventory can result in significant amounts of surplus equipment. All of these reductions in assets will generate substantial cash flow for a business, resulting in lower cost of capital and a healthier balance sheet. Another very valuable benefit of Lean is the simplicity that results. With processes shortened, they become easier to manage. In a Lean environment, scheduling is easy because the whole process is visible and products and processes can be pulled through the system at the desired pace.

Operating costs will decline significantly when non-value-added activities are reduced.

Lean processes can be a company's best sales tool. The ability to deliver a product quickly with no defects at a competitive price is crucial to today's competitive marketplace. The manufacturing floor can become a showplace for customers as well as a company's key to success.

Bottom-Up Management: Tool 2

Kaizen

Good Change
Harnessing creative energy

K aizen is a Japanese term that means continuous improvement. In its literal translation from Japanese, it means "small, ongoing good" (Kai) and "good, for the better" (zen). As practiced in the Western world, Kaizen is a technique for analyzing and improving processes; it is a highly valuable tool for implementing Lean and Bottom-Up Management.

When a company has determined its Vision and its strategies, Kaizen is a structured way to involve employees in determining the tactics to implement the strategies. While the Kaizen process can be utilized to solve virtually any problem in a business, or to generate new ideas, it is most effective in developing ideas for continuous improvement in productivity.

Kaizen is the ultimate Bottom-Up Management tool.

In North America, most Kaizen is practiced as part of a Kaizen event or blitz with a cross-functional team. Before any Kaizen event can proceed, the leaders of the company or division communicate clearly to the team in writing and orally the specific objectives assigned to the team and the extent of its authority (the team mandate). Any ambiguity or inconsistency will be detrimental to the team's chances of success. Kaizen events usually take place in an extremely short time period, seldom exceeding five days. They can result in important and rapid improvements.

Kaizen is the ultimate Bottom-Up Management tool. It empowers employees in a team format to help a company make

> *Managers who encourage the Kaizen process are invariably surprised by its effectiveness.*

improvements that enable it to move closer to its Vision. The process relies on the energy and creativity that arise from inspiring, informing and involving employees. Managers who encourage the Kaizen process are invariably surprised by its effectiveness.

The Kaizen Process
Bottom-Up Management at its best

The Kaizen process includes education, documentation, analysis, redesign, and implementation. All these steps are essential to its effectiveness.

Education

All Kaizen events need to be preceded by education. This starts with educating management so it is knowledgeable about Lean principles and the Kaizen process and is committed to them. Without enthusiastic management committed to the process, it has little chance of succeeding. The next step is to train Kaizen participants in the Lean principles and Kaizen process. The better part of the first day of most Kaizen events is typically devoted to this training. Most people are unfamiliar with the concepts; they must be given time to absorb the issues and develop buy-in.

robably the most unique aspect of ʿaizen events is the empowerment ssociated with them.

Documentation

The next task for the Kaizen team is the documentation and analysis of the process being studied. The first item that needs to be identified and documented is the takt time of the process in question. Once the takt is determined, the team can then focus on all other areas.

The rate at which the product or service is required is pivotal to visualizing an operation. The takt time is needed in order to determine the loads on individual functions or machines. It

Exhibit 3.2.1

Common Non-Value-Added Activities

Activity	Bucket of NVAs *(see tool 1)*	Example
Rework	Defects (#7)	Products not made to specification. Have to go back into plant for additional work
Duplication of effort	Waste in the work itself (#6)	Salesperson handwrites order, gives it to clerk who enters it into computer
Unnecessary activites	Waste in the work itself (#6)	Inspector checking part off-line that could have been checked in-line by operator
Unnecessary motion	Motion (#5)	Machine operator picks up part with left hand and switches to right hand to insert in machine
Products in queue	Waiting (#3)	Sheet steel blanked in large batches and then waiting to be moved to welding department
Travel	Transportation (#4)	Operator walking to tool crib
Setup/changeover	Waste in the work itself (#6)	Resetting machine to accomodate different part

becomes the guiding force when cellular processing is put into place. When takt time is not identified, companies can make incorrect decisions, which lead to unnecessary capital expenditures or dissatisfied customers.

Every action in the process, including waiting time, should be timed and recorded on a process documentation form. (See Appendix 3.) In the interest of time management, the Kaizen team is usually broken down into smaller sub-teams that focus on the documentation of sub-parts of the process.

When the documentation is complete, the Kaizen team should then review and analyze every step and determine if it is value-added or non-value-added. This activity usually takes some time and debate until the team has agreed on a consistent definition of value-added. Non-value-added activities should be broken down into the seven buckets described in Tool 1. (See Exhibit 3.2.1 for examples.)

Once the Kaizen team has categorized the complete process into value-added and non-value-added steps and their respective time requirements, they brainstorm to search for opportunities to:
• Reduce or eliminate NVAs
• Improve efficiency, reducing the cycle times of value-added activities.

When the team has broken the NVAs into their sub-types, they should then list the sub-types in descending order of NVA time. The team then turns its attention to exploring ways to reduce or eliminate the major NVA activities. Some might require minor changes to the process and others could involve major redesigns or layout changes. For example, a high error rate on a particular machine caused by the operator periodically inserting the part incorrectly could be eliminated. This could be achieved by building a fixture that prevents the part from being inserted incorrectly. (See Tool 1: Error Proofing.) In this situation, the team might ask the tool and die department 1 build the fixture. Alternatively, excessive distances travele by parts might contribu to excessive waiting ar travel time. The team mig redesign the manufacturir process to bring activiti closer together.

> Using the problem-solving talents of
> Kaizen teams to bring the benefits of
> Lean to a business is Bottom-Up
> Management at its best.

Implementation

Probably the most uniqu aspect of Kaizen events is the empowerment associated wi them. Teams are given specific mandates by their leaders a1 some are then given wide powers to redesign processes ar implement changes, without any additional approvals. . first, it seems reckless to managers when it is suggested th they assign so much leeway to Kaizen teams. However, it is t creativity generated by the confidence and trust of the comp ny's leaders that sparks breakthroughs. If a team learns that will be presenting the results of its work to leaders only aft the changes have been implemented, the initial reaction shock and nervousness quickly gives way to pride and a fe ing of ownership.

After sitting through their first Kaizen team post-implement tion presentation, very few leaders retain any doubts abo the wisdom or effectiveness of the Kaizen process. Most lea ers who start as skeptics become enthusiastic supporters.

It may be beneficial for companies beginning the Lean journ to appoint a director of continuous improvement. Kaizen pr ects need to have a champion to ensure that all items iden fied are completed in a timely fashion. The director also spe heads planning for future Kaizen events. Using the proble solving talents of in-house Kaizen teams to bring the benef of Lean to a business is Bottom-Up Management at its best

Bottom-Up Management: Tool 3

Real Accounting

RAAP with GAAP
Traditional accounting's failure

Accountants in the past have primarily focused on generating information in a standard format that meets generally accepted accounting principles, or GAAP. Although this information provides consistent and valuable information for shareholders, banks, suppliers and other business stakeholders, it does little for the people who need to measure performance and make critical decisions for a business.

In today's highly competitive environment, information is one of the most essential Bottom-Up Management tools. Because what gets measured gets improved, team leaders and their members throughout any organization need relevant and timely information about materials or processes. This information enables them to gauge their performance and implement improvements. They need what we call RAAP, or Real-time, Activity-based, Accountability-focused Performance data in addition to traditional GAAP information.

AAP accounting does little for the peo- ᵉ who need to measure performance •d make critical decisions for a business.

Real-Time Information
Speed up the cycle of learning

The shorter the time frame between business activity and information that measures or reports its result, the more valuable the information. Financial reporting in a GAAP format is generally received on a monthly, quarterly or annual basis. Even in businesses that diligently produce monthly GAAP information, the information is already four to six weeks out of date by the time it is received. Providing statements to managers or teams that tell them that they did not meet their goals weeks earlier is of limited value.

Real-time information prescribes that leaders and team members receive vital information as close to an event as possible. In this type of environment, information is often received in minutes, hours or at the latest, the next day.

The shorter the time frame between business activity and information that measures or reports its result, the more valuable the information.

Obtaining information in these periods greatly enhances the cycle of learning and is critical to maintaining focus on how the firm is performing relative to its objectives. When leaders and their team members get rapid feedback, they quickly learn what is working and what needs adjustment, as they experiment with different approaches. Armed with confidence about the likely outcome, they are able to make regular improvements to the process.

Timely and accurate feedback about how the firm is performing relative to stated objectives can be provided to leaders and employees in the form of flash reports. These reports circulated throughout the company communicate progress versus the targets for each driver of success. The flash reports should provide employees with the essential information needed to assess and improve their performance. (A sample flash report is provided in Appendix 4 and an hourly tracking chart is provided in Appendix 5.)

When leaders and their team members get rapid feedback, they quickly learn what is working and what needs adjustment

Used in a constructive manner, the flash report is the keystone element of the execution plan. It provides real-time outcomes of the daily activities designed to deliver results.

Activity-Based Costing: ABC
The real costs

GAAP financial statements are prepared using full-absorption accounting. Under this system, accountants allocate general types of overhead costs to the cost of products or services. While this works well for financial accounting issues, it often provides misleading information for management decisions.

The allocation process[1] can be arbitrary and lead to incorrect conclusions about the real cost of products or services. Significant and growing portions of a modern company's costs are allocated based on factors that are now obsolete because of new production technologies. Allocations are also very dependent on budgeted activity levels, which seldom occur as expected, causing further errors in cost estimates.

Traditional GAAP accounting can provide misleading information, which may result in incorrect judgments and decisions.

Activity-based costing, also known as ABC, was developed in the late 1980s. It is the actual cost of a product or service based on the activities that are directly involved in the development, production and delivery of the product or service. This approach places little or no reliance on allocations. The focus is to identify all the activities in a process and then determine the total of their costs.

Full-absorption accounting often uses direct labor as a critical

---

1. Allocations are often based on an estimate of sales, assets, square footage, direct labor or machine time.

benchmark for its calculations. As a result, all labor that is not considered direct is lumped in with overhead costs and becomes part of the allocation process. Direct labor, as it is applied in full-absorption accounting, has become a relatively small percentage of total cost in today's efficient and often-automated businesses. When allocation decisions are made based on a minor part of the cost equation, significant errors may result.

With ABC, the concept of direct labor and its distinction from indirect labor is less important; the focus is on capturing and measuring all labor and other costs in a process. An estimator who spends time on a quote or an engineer who is designing a modification to the product to meet the customer's needs is looked at in the same light as direct labor in an ABC environment.

ABC places variable costs on a higher level of importance than those that are fixed.

With full-absorption accounting, these costs can easily be ignored because they are lumped in with general overheads allocated to all products or jobs in an indiscriminate way. ABC is more precise, assigning costs to the actual department or product that caused them to occur. ABC gives leaders and their team members an effective Bottom-Up Management tool: a significantly more accurate assessment of the costs of a product or service. This approach provides the ability to make better resource allocation and strategic and pricing decisions.

Another valuable feature of ABC (and a differentiator from full-absorption accounting) is the separation of variable and fixed costs. Variable costs are those expenditures that tend to occur in proportion to sales. Fixed costs are those that do not vary with sales, tending to remain unchanged when sales volumes fluctuate.

Rent is a classic example of a fixed cost, unless sales grow so much that the business needs to move to larger premises. In most situations, a monthly fluctuation in sales volume will not result in a change in the company's rent expense.[2] The cost of raw materials, on the other hand, is usually a variable cost because the quantity of raw materials consumed relates directly to the volume of sales.[3]

Interestingly, many costs are not as variable as they might initially indicate. Direct labor is one expense category easily considered variable. On closer examination, however, most businesses find that there is often not a direct correlation between sales and direct labor. If sales decline, it is not necessarily easy to achieve a similar decline in direct labor because businesses need a core group of workers regardless of the sales level. On the other hand, when sales increase, businesses often experience an increase in productivity that reduces the need for a proportionate increase in direct labor.

ABC places variable costs on a higher level of importance than those that are fixed. The logic for this prioritizing is that variable costs involve incremental, discretionary expenditures. Fixed expenses, on the other hand, are not discretionary in the short term and cannot be easily avoided. Any action that would incur a variable cost should be examined very carefully. Will the expenditure generate the appropriate payback?

ABC first defines the extent of the variable costs, determined on an ABC basis, for a product or service to determine if the revenue it generates exceeds such cost. Then ABC calculates whether the amount of such excess (known as the variable contribution margin) will be sufficient to cover the attributa-

2. Exception: Rent agreements which have a "Percentage Rent" clause, which ties rent expense to sales volumes. These agreements are quite common in retail malls.
3. Exception: A company increasing its levels of inventory, in which case it might be using materials disproportionate to the sales level.

ble and non-attributable fixed costs as well as the desired profit margin. (Non-attributable costs cannot be determined to be directly applied to or related to a specific product; for example, insurance[4] and utilities.)

Activity-based costing takes considerably more effort than full-absorption accounting, sometimes requiring exhaustive searches and analyses, such as time-and-motion studies. The effort is usually worthwhile because team leaders and members are armed with more accurate cost information, allowing better pricing and strategic decisions.

4.   Exception: Insurance costs that are directly related to direct labor (workers' compensation) or product liability if it is based on a percentage of sales.

Exhibit 3.3.1

Using Variable Costing and Activity-Based Costing to Make Operating Decisions

	Products			
	A	B	C	Total
Sales Revenue	$ 1,000	$ 3,000	$ 5,000	$ 9,000
Variable Costs	600	2,250	2,500	5,350
Variable Contribution Margin	400	750	2,500	3,650
	40%	25%	50%	41%
Fixed Costs – Attributable	500	330	600	1,430
Product Profit Margin	(100)	420	1,900	2,220
	-10%	14%	38%	24%
Fixed Costs– Non-Attributable				1,500
Profit Margin				$ 720
				8%
Profit Goal				15%

Making the Right Decisions with ABC
Turning accounting into a competitive weapon

The following examples demonstrate the difference between activity-based costing and full-absorption accounting.

In Exhibit 3.3.1, a business is pursing three product lines. All variable costs are determined using ABC, arriving at the variable contribution margin by deducting the variable costs from the sales revenue. The product profit margin is then determined by deducting those fixed costs that can be specifically attributed (as differentiated from allocated) to the product.

ABC is not accounting gymnastics; it can highlight serious flaws in the company's information systems and decision-making process.

For example, an engineer who works only on Product A could represent a fixed cost attributable to that product. The non-attributable fixed costs (examples: legal expenses, accounting department, management compensation) are then deducted in total to arrive at the net profit margin for the business as a whole.

In Exhibit 3.3.2, costs for the same products are calculated using full-absorption accounting. This method differs in two material aspects that could result in serious errors in the decision-making process because of inadequate information. In this example, full-absorption accounting has not separately identified fixed costs and has allocated total fixed costs based on sales revenue.

With the ABC approach (Exhibit 3.3.1), fixed costs are specifically attributed to products. The result is a disproportionately high amount of costs being attributed to Product A, revealing that this product has a negative product profit margin even before taking into account non-attributable fixed costs.

When all of the fixed costs (attributable and non-attributable) are allocated on a full-absorption accounting basis as indicated in the second example (Exhibit 3.3.2), one ninth of $2,930 or $325 has been allocated to Product A. That amount deducted from the variable contribution margin of $400 reflects a misleading net profit of $75. This comparison demonstrates the potential inadequacy of full-absorption accounting.

Many businesses walk away from lucrative potential business because their accounting system gives them misleading information.

It is also important to note that ABC reflects that Product B is generating a significant product profit margin of $420. However, with full-absorption accounting, when the fixed costs are allocated, $975 (33%) would be allocated to Product B, indicating a loss of $225.

This is not accounting gymnastics; these different methods of analysis can have a material impact on business decisions. If Product A is pursued, the business will lose money, even though full-absorption accounting indicates that the product is profitable. Product B, on the other hand, is clearly profitable, but could have been judged unprofitable utilizing full-absorption accounting.

Product A reflects a negative product profit margin in ABC because a large amount of fixed costs can be attributed to it. In fact, Product A is generating an attractive variable contri-

Exhibit 3.3.2

Using Full-Absorption Accounting to Make Operating Decisions

Products			
A	**B**	**C**	**Total**

	A	B	C	Total
Sales Revenue	$ 1,000	$ 3,000	$ 5,000	$ 9,000
Variable Costs	600	2,250	2,500	5,350
Variable Contribution Margin	400	750	2,500	3,650
	40%	25%	50%	41%
Fixed Costs – Allocated on Sales	325	975	1,630	2,930
Product Profit Margin	75	(225)	870	720
Profit Margin	8%	(8%)	17%	8%
Profit Goal				15%

bution margin of 40%. Before concluding that this product is detrimental to the business's future, leaders should consider some strategic alternatives.

If, for example, sales revenue of this product could be grown to $2,000, its product profit margin, after attributable fixed costs of $500 (which should not change because they are fixed), could grow to a positive $300 ($2,000 multiplied by 40% minus $500). This is the kind of valuable information, derived from variable costing and ABC, which facilitates better decision making.

Variable costing and ABC also facilitate more accurate and appropriate pricing decisions. Many businesses walk away from lucrative potential business because their accounting system gives them misleading information.

Team leaders and members must have the correct Bottom-Up Management tools to make decisions. Knowing the real costs puts them in a position to help the company succeed. Without this vital information, the business is using guesswork to make decisions.

Accountability
Stepping up to the plate

Accountability is vitally important for making a Vision a reality. Tasks must be broken down into bite-sized pieces with individuals or teams held accountable for results. Without this structure, success will be jeopardized.

To support the focus on accountability, information systems have to provide the data needed to measure performance against goals. This includes:

- Comprehensive budgets, comparison to actual performance and analysis of the differences
- Accurate and up-to-date financial standards
- Statements of operations and balance sheets (actual and budget) broken down by division, department and product line, preferably prepared using variable and activity-based costing
- Timely financial information, preferably daily and weekly, reflecting drivers of success (flash reports)

True accountability goes beyond holding individual employees to appropriate performance standards. Divisions, departments, product lines, individual products and even businesses as a whole need to held accountable for clearly defined responsibilities. Goals and objectives must be set and reviewed regularly. Compensation programs should be significantly impacted by these reviews.

Accountability is a vital key to successful TDVBUM. Without being able to break a task down into bite-sized pieces, measure performance and hold people and teams accountable for

Without accountability, all the pressure for achieving the Vision is on the CEO's shoulders.

their responsibilities, all of the pressure for achieving the Vision is on the CEO's shoulders.

Accountability must be accompanied by authority. Even the best manager is unable to be effective without the authority to ensure that tasks are properly executed.

Performance Data
Information for making decisions

The only information many businesses receive is pure financial data. For smaller or medium-sized companies, the production of this information is often the responsibility of the accounting department or the independent accountant. In most situations, this type of financial information does not provide appropriate information for operating decision making.

In order to turn a business Vision into reality, it is essential to provide leaders and team members with operational data. This information helps them judge their operating performance and allows them to make and measure improvements. Providing this data quickly increases its value significantly.

Examples of performance data include:
- Orders received
- Production results
- Shipments
- Productivity
- Overtime
- Scrap
- Rework
- Raw material yields
- Equipment utilization
- Setup times
- Inventory turnover rates
- Accounts receivable collection rates
- Product or service costs
- Gross profit margins
- Variable contribution margin

Providing information about business performance to management and employees pays handsome dividends.

As discussed earlier, data must be provided on a timely and regular basis to leaders and team members throughout the company to let them know how they are performing against the goals. One of the most valuable tools is the flash report. (See Appendix 4.)

Bottom-Up Management: Tool 4

Brainstorming and Analytical Techniques

Brainstorming
Strength in numbers

The effectiveness and value of Top-Down Vision and Bottom-Up Management is built on the principle that group dynamics and brainstorming, properly structured and implemented, produce more creativity and buy-in than generating ideas individually. The power of brainstorming lies in developing ideas in a group situation based on the principles of suspended judgment and cross-stimulation. Participants' diverse thinking habits and pool of knowledge and experience make brainstorming a creative and highly valuable Bottom-Up Management tool.

Consider an example of brainstorming power. In a training session with a client, we selected a random person on the team. She was given a paper clip and asked to write down on a piece of paper different uses for the paper clip. She was allowed 45 seconds. We then asked the team to brainstorm aloud the uses they could think of, which were written on the board. They were allowed 30 seconds. Then the two approaches were compared. The team thought of 50 percent more uses than the individual, in one-third less time. The result of this exercise highlights the power of many minds versus one.

Group dynamics and brainstorming, properly structured and implemented, produce more creativity and buy-in than generating ideas individually.

While there are several ground rules or suggestions for an effective brainstorming session, one is primary: no evaluation of ideas from one's peers. It is imperative for the facilitator of the group to make participants feel comfortable

Brainstorming is a unique opportunity to make suggestions that people ordinarily would not make.

expressing their ideas without fear of criticism or ridicule. Brainstorming is a unique opportunity to make suggestions that people ordinarily would not make.

The facilitator must stress that no idea is too absurd. People should not even evaluate their own ideas or the novelty of an idea; sometimes resurrecting an idea can be effective. As a good warm-up exercise for the meeting, the facilitator can suggest a foolish idea as a solution to an unrelated problem and ask people to identify the advantages of the flawed idea. After everyone offers suggestions, participants will be more willing to reveal ideas, expecting not to be criticized.

The facilitator should stress that the wilder the ideas, the better; it is also valuable to encourage building on ideas of others rather than just suggesting new ideas. Building on previously suggested ideas compliments the author of the idea and pushes wild concepts toward practicality. Brainstorming sessions often reward people for individual submissions, steering energy into new concepts rather than building on the old. The facilitator can help lead the group away from this tendency. Even ideas that are misunderstood can still be used as a stimulus. In addition, what may seem obvious and trivial can result in original ideas when combined with others.

The initial session should focus on getting comfortable with the principles and methods of brainstorming and the mandate or task. At the next session, participants should focus on listing all their ideas about the task. Later, the same group should get together and sift through the list of ideas that they generated to find the useful ones. Something useful can be extracted from even the ridiculous ideas. The group might have three lists in which to place the remaining ideas – ideas of immediate usefulness, areas for further exploration and new approaches to the problem.

A facilitator, who should not be controlling, is needed to lay down the ground rules and guide the group. It is important to formulate a problem/objective at the beginning of the session that is not so broad that it brings too many ideas, but also not so narrow that it restricts ideas. Participants should all agree that only one person talks at a time. The facilitator can and should ask questions to provoke thought and discussion. He/she also organizes the evaluation session and the list of ideas.

A note taker is needed to make a permanent list of all of the ideas, omitting none, no matter how off-the-wall they seem. The note taker should make sufficient notes to understand the ideas out of context in subsequent sessions. The note taker also decides if an idea is too similar to a previous idea on the list.

One hour is ideal for a brainstorming session, although it can be anywhere from thirty to 120 minutes. It is better to stop while ideas are still being generated and have participants submit a list of additional ideas after the session. The group can range in size from six to fifteen, but ten to twelve members are ideal. Less than six generates arguments and does not create enough ideas and more than fifteen does not allow everyone to contribute. If there are more than fifteen participants, people can be broken into groups and notes can be compared.

Several tools can be used while brainstorming or in place of brainstorming that help achieve the desired result. Some of these are listed and described in the following chapters.

Exhibit 3.4.1

Fishbone Diagram

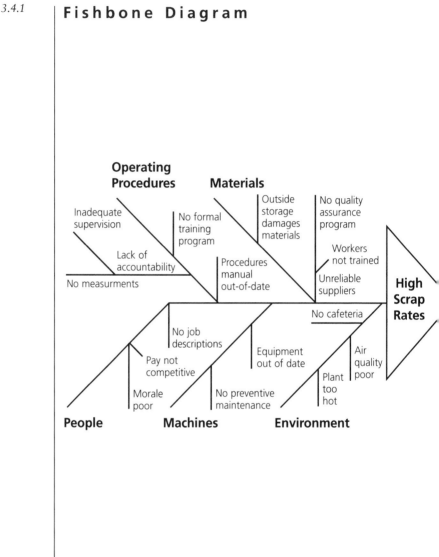

Fishbone Diagrams
Addressing causes, not symptoms

The fishbone diagram is an analytical tool that provides a methodical way of looking at effects and the causes that create or contribute to those effects. The design of the diagram resembles a fish skeleton. It is often called a cause-and-effect diagram or an Ishikawa diagram, after its founder Dr. Kaoru Ishikawa, a Japanese quality-control statistician. The fishbone diagram helps teams categorize the many potential causes of problems or issues in an orderly way and identify root causes.

The fishbone diagram helps teams categorize the many potential causes of problems or issues in an orderly way and identify root causes.

A fishbone diagram is most helpful when:
- You want to study all the possible reasons that a process is beginning to have problems or breakdowns
- You need to study a problem or issue to determine the root cause
- You want to understand why a process is not performing properly or producing the desired results

Below is an outline of how to create the fishbone diagram:
1. Draw the fishbone diagram (see Exhibit 3.4.1).
2. List the problem/issue to be studied in the "head of the fish."
3. Label each "bone" of the "fish." The major categories typically are:

The four Ms: Methods, Machines, Materials, Manpower
The four Ps: Place, Procedure, People, Policies
The four Ss: Surroundings, Suppliers, Systems, Skills
Note: You may use one of the three categories suggested *combine them in any fashion or make up your own. The* *categories are to help you organize your ideas.*

4. Use an idea-generating technique (for example, brain storming) to identify the factors within each category tha may be affecting the problem/issue and/or effect being studied. The team shoul ask, "What are the machine issues affecting /causing...?"

A fishbone diagram is most helpful when you want to study all the possible reasons that a process is beginning to have problems or breakdowns.

5. Repeat this procedure with each factor unde the category to produce sub-factors. Continue asking, "Why is this happening?" and put additional segments under each fac tor and sub-factor.

6. Continue until you no longer get useful information.

7. Analyze the results of the fishbone after team members agree that an adequate amount of detail has been provided under each major category. Look for items that appear in more than one category. These become the most likely causes.

8. For those items identified as the most likely causes, the team should reach consensus on listing those items in priority order, with the first item being the most probable cause.

Storyboarding
Visual brainstorming

Storyboarding is a technique used to organize and display information and brainstorm ideas. It can take many different forms; our recommended method uses storyboarding to enhance the group process to solve a problem visually as a team.

Storyboarding is used to:
- Encourage divergent thinking
- Display information visually
- Organize problem solving
- Develop team consensus
- Generate a plan of action

Storyboarding enhances the group process to solve a problem visually as a team.

Storyboarding works best with a small group, typically five to eight people. Larger groups can be divided into smaller groups. A quiet, comfortable room with clear walls so papers and cards of all sizes can be pinned or taped to them is essential. The group needs a large quantity of cards or heavy paper in many sizes and colors, a couple of rolls of masking tape or pins and enough marking pens for everyone. It is very important to have a skilled facilitator whom participants recognize as fair and unbiased.

Storyboarding Steps
1. **State the problem or objective.** The group facilitator begins by stating the problem and the objectives to be accomplished clearly and concisely.

Exhibit 3.4.2

Listing Possible Causes of a Problem

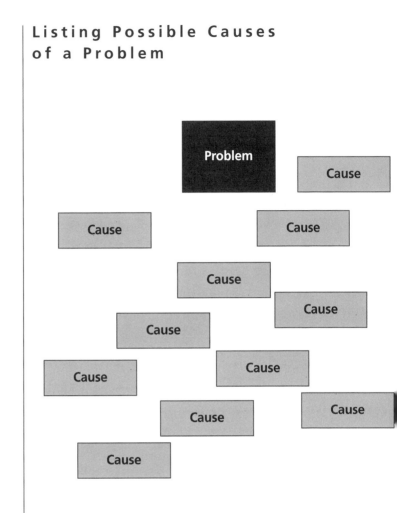

2. **Brainstorm and post all ideas**. Participants work quietly by themselves for about 10 minutes, writing down possible solutions to the stated problem. Each idea is written in large letters on a separate card or piece of paper. As in brainstorming, the quantity of ideas is what is important at this stage in the process. The group facilitator will pick up the cards/papers and tape them to the wall.

3. **Share ideas**. Participants talk about what they have writ-

Categorizing Causes of a Problem

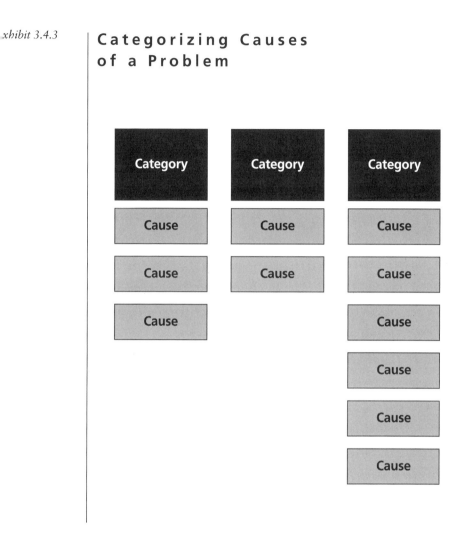

ten on the cards. This discussion should generate more ideas, encouraging group thinking.

4. **Review each card for meaning.** After the brainstorming period, participants should take a few minutes to look at all of the items posted on the wall. Participants can ask for clarification on unclear items. It is important for the group to understand the meaning of every card.

5. **Sort by content.** The group should then go to the wall

Exhibit 3.4.4

Prioritizing Causes of a Problem

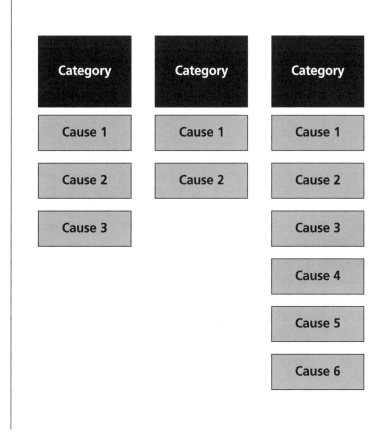

and begin sorting and grouping the items of similar content. People should be encouraged to observe and suggest changes or additions to the groupings.

6. **Add header cards.** Participants are then given several "header cards" that are of a different color and larger than the idea cards previously used. These cards are used to create categories or groups into which many of the cards will fall.

7. **Discuss the groupings.** After the header cards are placed on the wall, the facilitator asks the group how it feels about the headings and the content. There may be a need to break some of the topics into sub-topics with subtitles.

8. **Symptoms vs. causes.** Once the group feels comfortable with the way the cards are sorted, participants should step back and consider what they have identified as key issues or ideas. Sound decision-making is based on identifying the root causes of the problem, not symptoms. The focus should be on the factors that are actually responsible for creating the original problem. The group may want to add, rewrite, or rearrange the cards to focus more accurately on the root causes.

9. **Vote for consensus.** The group identifies the top three or four ideas. If there is not a clear consensus, it uses a multi-voting process. Each participant votes for ideas on the wall using the following points:
   - 4 votes for first choice
   - 3 votes for second choice
   - 2 votes for third choice
   - 1 vote for fourth choice

10. **Restate header cards using a verb.** Examine each header card and restate it as an action item. In other words, replace a noun with a verb.

11. **Sub-tier actions.** If sub-tier actions are necessary, post them under the header cards.

12. **Assign completion dates.** Assign a completion date to each item.

13. **Post dates and names.** Post dates and the name of the person responsible for each action item.

Consensus Building
Finding common ground

Reaching consensus is a group process in which every participant's input is carefully considered and an outcome is crafted to meet the needs of the group. It is a process of synthesizing all participants' wisdom into the best decision possible at the time. The root of consensus is the word consent, which means to give permission. Someone may disagree with the decision, but all individuals agree to let the group's decision go forward.

The heart of consensus building is a cooperative intent. Key attributes to successful participation include willingness to listen to others and see their perspectives, and willingness to share one's own ideas, but not insist that they are the best ones.

The benefits include:
1. **Consensus gathers the experiences of the entire group.** Within every member of any group, there is a lifetime of experiences and knowledge. Consensus is a way to tap the collective knowledge of the group to create the best decision possible.
2. **Consensus builds relationships.** In a consensus process, people extend their relationships as part of the listening and talking process. Consensus takes time, effort, honest communication and a willingness to trust the relationship. Communicating ideas and feelings, and listening empathetically build trust and bond group members. By encouraging shared leadership and participation, consensus empowers all the members of a group to help make the best decision. The synergy of building

collaborative agreements builds a strong sense of belonging and commitment to the group and its mission

3. **Consensus moves toward doing what is best for the common interest.** The key element of making consensus work is a commitment by each individual to honor the best interests of the group. As people work through issues, they have their own needs reflected back to them in the context of the larger group needs. This encourages them to consider other interests beyond their own.

4. **Consensus agreements need less enforcement.** When everyone gives consent to an agreement, it is backed by the relationship. If people honor their relationship to the group, their respect for the agreements that they participated in guides them to follow the agreement. Agreements made by consensus are self-enforced and rarely require anything more than a reminder to ensure compliance.

The Three Stages of Consensus Building

Discussion Stage - The group starts by discussing and agreeing on its objectives. It then holds broad discussions on the topic. People freely share opinions, feelings and ideas and react to each other's contributions. This is the heart of consensus because it is where people come together and synthesize thoughts. This is where opinions, if already formed, are subject to change as people hear other perspectives.

Consensus is a way to tap the collective knowledge of the group to create the best decision possible.

Proposal Stage - Ideas are synthesized into one or more proposal statements. This is where good facilitators add value because they look for the common areas of understanding and agreement. They bring those out and summarize them for the group. As common ground emerges from the discussion, it is captured in writing.

Modification Stage - The summary proposal is tested and modified to meet the needs of the group. In some cases, modification is done at the same meeting. In other situations, it is done weeks after the meeting, as the decision is implemented and things are learned from the experience. The decision is reviewed and amended as new information becomes available.

How do you know you have consensus?

When all the participants give permission for the proposal to go ahead, consensus is reached. Typically, the facilitator will ask the group for an affirmation of the proposal and at that time, everyone signals consent.

How to deal with lack of consensus

It is rare that consensus is achieved right away. Even if the majority of the people reach consensus, there will often be some who will express concern or discomfort with the idea or proposal under discussion. A team may erroneously be tempted to try to persuade the holdouts to come around to the majority's point of view. Instead, it should view the dissenting opinions as an opportunity to reexamine the fundamental merits of its position.

Minority opinions should be respected and seen as an opportunity to put a concept through its paces. If this is done, the majority is often surprised to find out that there is merit in such concerns. Teams that conduct themselves in this manner always achieve better results.

Exhibit 3.4.5

M i n d   M a p p i n g

Property Management Company Converting from
Warehouse to site delivery

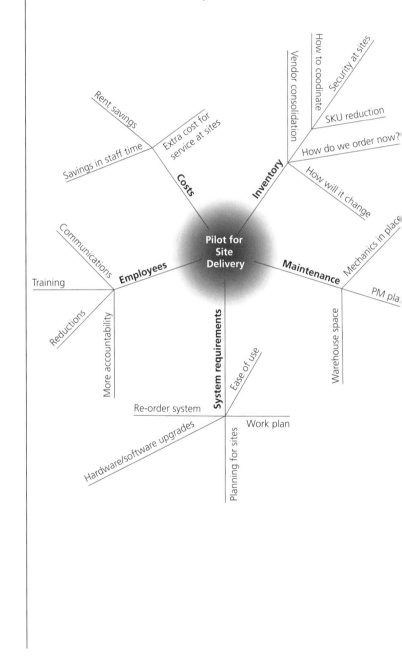

Mind Mapping®
Unlocking the brain

T he Mind Map® is an expression of Radiant Thinking®[1] and is therefore a natural function of the human mind. It is a powerful graphic technique that provides a universal key to unlocking the potential of the brain. (See Exhibit 3.4.5.) The Mind Map can be applied to every aspect of life where improved learning and clearer thinking will enhance human performance. The Mind Map has four essential characteristics:

- The subject of attention is crystallized in a central image
- The main themes of the subject radiate from the central image on branches
- Branches hold a key image/word printed on the associated line, with details radiating outward
- The branches form a connected nodal structure

Group Mind Mapping
Mind Maps are an excellent vehicle for effective work in groups. There are several different ways groups can use Mind Maps. One is a process called "brain blooming," an alternative to brainstorming. The steps are as follows:

- Use a Mind Map to capture each individual's thoughts.
- Blend thoughts from a small group.
- Discuss the basic layout of the Mind Map. During the initial stage, all ideas should be accepted.
- Combine all small-group Mind Maps into one large Mind Map for a true representation of the group's thinking.
- Have a miscellaneous branch for ideas that do not fit

---

1. Mind Maps and Radiant Thinking are registered trademarks of The Buzan Group, 1990. The Mind Mapping concept was developed by Tony Buzan.

anywhere else to ensure that all ideas are captured.

There are a number of advantages of group Mind Mapping over brainstorming:
- Each person has thinking time to generate his/her own ideas.
- The ideas are given equal weight and a layout that captures the meaning of all concepts is agreed upon.
- The radiant hierarchy means judging is reduced.
- Ideas are grouped on the main theme branches.
- Connections may be seen between branches and ideas.

The Mind Map can be applied to every aspect of life where improved learning and clearer thinking will enhance human performance.

One of our project managers recently used mind mapping to help coordinate a project for a property management company that involved switching from a warehousing operation to JIT site delivery. Accomplishing this mission will save the company more than thirty percent in operating funds and improve cash flow. The project will be launched at a pilot site to test and refine the new system. The project manager used mind mapping to brainstorm potential problems and generate ideas for improving the pilot. Exhibit 3.4.5 shows the mind map created to help sort out priorities.

Exhibit 3.4.6

The Change Loop

		Rank	Difficulty	Impact
A	Everyone smiles	3-8	Low	Low
B	Leadership Focus	2-4	Medium	High
C	Zero defects	0-6	High	High
D	We have process control	2	Medium	High
E	We measure visually	0-5	Low	Medium
F	We are reliable	0-6	Low	Medium
G	Customers prefer our products	5-7	High	High
H	We command a premium price	2-7	High	High
J	Pro-active engagement with customers	2-8	Low	Medium
K	Our workforce is empowered	2-4	Low	High
L	Employees take pride	3-8	Low	High
M	We actively communicate	0-5	Low	High
N	We deliver all products on time	2-4	Medium	High

High			C,G,H
Medium			B,D,N
Low A		E,F,J	K,L,M
	Low	**Medium**	**High**

Difficulty

Impact

The Change Loop
What's first?

The change loop is a process that helps to identify the key initiatives that will improve a company, the difficulty in implementing them and the potential impact of their implementation. Once the difficulty and impact of an initiative are determined, the initiatives can be analyzed on a matrix that makes it easy to see what initiatives to work on first.

Initiatives can be analyzed on a matrix that makes it easy to see what initiatives to work on first.

Process example

- In a brainstorming session that focuses on a specific topic (examples: quality, customer satisfaction), ask the group, "What does 'good' (quality) look like?"
- Ask all participants to express what they believe good (quality) looks like. The facilitator should record all of the answers.
- Have everyone privately rate where the company currently is on a scale of one to ten (one being poor and ten being excellent) in each of these categories. Tally the results and write the range of answers next to each category.
- Using the group for input, rank each category in difficulty of completion and impact of completion in the next two columns. Categories are ranked low, medium or high.
- Graph in a matrix format (see Exhibit 3.4.6).

The initiatives in the bottom right corner of the matrix (low difficulty, high impact) should be implemented as soon as possible. The other initiatives should be reviewed to decide which ones add the most value.

Exhibit 3.4.7

Pareto Analysis

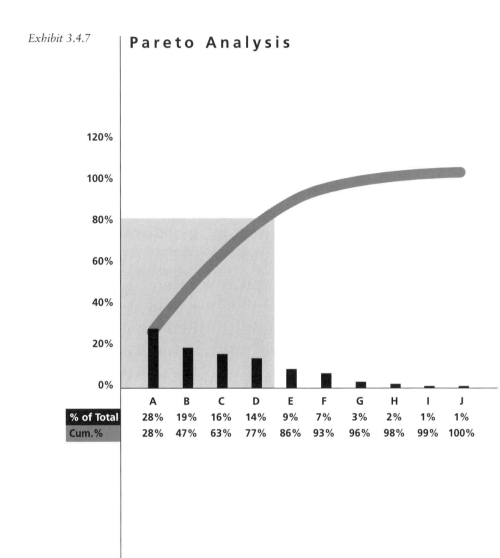

	A	B	C	D	E	F	G	H	I	J
% of Total	28%	19%	16%	14%	9%	7%	3%	2%	1%	1%
Cum.%	28%	47%	63%	77%	86%	93%	96%	98%	99%	100%

Pareto Analysis
Focus quickly

The Pareto Principle states that only a few factors are responsible for producing most problems. This principle can be applied toward improving quality. (See discussion of the 80:20 rule in Strategies, Part II.) By identifying the issues that are most important, the team can quickly focus its efforts on the key causes of a problem. The Pareto analysis presents conclusions in an easy-to-interpret graphic format.

Process
- Complete a cause-and-effect analysis (see Fishbone Diagrams chapter, above). Once the possible causes of a problem have been identified, complete a study that determines the number of times each cause appears in a given time period.
- Rank the causes from the most to the least prevalent and calculate the cumulative percentage.
- Draw a horizontal axis (X) that represents the different causes, ordered from the most to least frequent.
- Draw a vertical axis (Y) with percentages from zero to 100%.
- Construct a bar graph based on the percentage of each cause.
- Construct a line graph of the cumulative percent.
- Draw a line from 80% on the Y-axis to the line graph, and then drop the line down to the X-axis. This line separates the important causes from the trivial ones.

By identifying the issues that are most important, the team can quickly focus its efforts on the key causes of a problem.

Facilitation Techniques and Skills
Productive meetings

Because of the importance of group dynamics and brainstorming to the TDVBUM process, many people in the organization need to become effective facilitators to ensure that team meetings are productive and successful. The following good practices support effective facilitation:

1. **Prepare** – Pre-meeting checklist
   - Create an agenda.
   - Set the meeting place and be sure to reserve it.
   - Comfortable seating with water is preferable.
   - Send invitations with the agenda to all desired participants.
   - Prepare the meeting room before everyone's arrival. Be sure there are enough seats, you have the right equipment and there is no glare from windows.

2. **Begin** – Focusing everyone on the task at hand
   - Discuss the purpose/goal of the meeting.
   - Review the agenda.
   - Establish and agree on ground rules.
   - Ask a warm-up question to encourage participation, focus the group on the subject and gauge opinions. (Example: How do you feel about being on this team and what is your initial reaction to the team mandate?)

3. **Inform** – Help the group understand the background using:
   - Historical timelines
   - SWOT Analysis
   - Porter's Five Forces

4. **Gather Information** – Ask the group to think of possible approaches to solving the problem.
   - Challenge assumptions and ask "Why?"

- Brainstorm, using techniques described above.
5. **Build Consensus** – Reach an agreement on settling the problem.
   - Set criteria for decision making.
   - Weigh pros and cons.
   - Vote.
6. **Plan and Implement** – Develop an action plan
   - Assign action items: what to be done, when and by whom.
   - Schedule another meeting.
7. **Close** – End meeting and gain perspective.
   - Summarize.
   - Ask for feedback on open issues.
   - Solicit group feedback on success of meeting.
   - Adjourn.
8. **Follow Up** – Distribute the minutes or key information within 24 hours.

Skills of an Effective Facilitator
An effective facilitator can:
- Plan and organize
- Listen actively
- Build and sustain a supportive environment
- Handle differences constructively
- Deal effectively with dysfunctional behavior:
  - Rambling – Thank person for participation and ask how it relates to the current subject.
  - Argumentative – Stay calm, finding merit in their thoughts or use humor and move on.
  - Dominating – Ask a difficult question or thank person and move on.
  - Inarticulate – Help paraphrase.
  - Side conversations – Pause and look at the offenders and/or ask them to share.
- Summarize and paraphrase
  - "So you're saying…"

- "So you mean…"
- "Let me see if I understood…"

Sample Ground Rules for Meetings
- Have a facilitator or leader.
- Start and end on time.
- If unable to attend or need to leave early, notify the leader or send a representative.
- Leader and participants are prepared.
- Distribute the agenda.
- Follow the prepared agenda.
- Respect everyone's input/opinion.
- No side conversations.
- No distracting or dysfunctional behavior.
- Everyone has an opportunity to participate.
- Treat discussions as confidential until team agrees on method and time to share with the rest of the organization.
- Distribute the minutes to participants with a list of action items, dates and owners.
- Many people in the organization need to become effective facilitators to ensure that team meeting are productive and successful.

Many people in the organization need to become effective facilitators to ensure that team meetings are productive and successful.

Bottom-Up Management: Tool 5

Gainsharing

Laser Focus
Shared goals and rewards

N o business can rely on compensation alone to motivate employees. Creating an incentive program that rewards everyone in the company for the improvements that move the business toward its goals can be very helpful. When employees are inspired by the company's Vision, their own empowerment and opportunity for advancement, there is a healthy environment. Attempting to make up for workplace shortcomings with financial incentives usually provides disappointing and short-lived results.

A gainsharing plan should be viewed as a way for everyone in the company to become laser-focused on achieving the company's goals.

Reward systems for employees that are consistent with the long-term interests of the organization can be very beneficial to the company and its employees. These types of incentive programs are known as gainsharing plans. A gainsharing plan should not be viewed as a "carrot" to get people to do what the company wants them to do. Rather, it is a way for everyone in the company to become laser-focused on achieving the company's goals.

A gainsharing plan that is based on achieving the Vision and its goals sends a very clear message to all employees: "These are our goals. We want and need every employee dedicated to achieving them and we will all be able to share in the rewards of success."

Incentive Compensation Plan Considerations
Shared destiny

At their core, incentive compensation plans (ICPs) are intended to spur employees to engage in activities that are required for an organization to achieve its objectives. Effective ICPs are not measured by employees' activities, but by the results of their work.

An incentive compensation plan must be relevant, understandable, timely and fair.

ICPs work within solid compensation plans, so that when the results of employees' actions are aligned with expectations, employees receive rewards for engaging in those actions. When those actions produce results that exceed expectations, rewards are greater than normal. On the other hand, when results fall short, the economic rewards are reduced or even eliminated. In order to be effective, an incentive plan must be relevant, understandable, timely and fair.

Relevant
The incentives being offered must make sense in the context of the needs of the employees. For example, providing free parking as an incentive for employees who are not being paid enough to afford an automobile does not constitute an effective motivator, even though the cost is still there for the employer. In addition, incentive compensation payments that represent a small percentage of an employee's base pay result in compensation disparity and are not effective incentives. Employees must find the incentive rewards worth seeking.

Understandable
Employees must understand how their behavior directly affects the rewards they can receive from the incentive program. If a plan is so complex that employees cannot understand how it will affect them, it does not provide any incentive for change.

Timely
To be effective, rewards earned from the incentive plan must be distributed as soon as possible. This reinforces the link between behavior and rewards for that behavior.

The most effective structure for an ICP is the shared-destiny approach.

Fair
With well-designed ICPs, plan participants feel that they are being treated in a manner that gives no one an unfair advantage or disadvantage. ICPs that are team-based tend to be more productive. ICPs based on individuals acting for their own benefit are often divisive and destructive to the long-term culture and performance of an organization.

The most effective structure for an ICP is the shared-destiny approach. In this approach, all employees share in the rewards for achieving a desired outcome; the varying amounts they receive reflect the impact they have on the organization. All too often, traditional bonus plans are based on subjective measures that require a judgment by a third party, who may or may not be objective. That practice drives a stake in the heart of a good ICP.

Communication
Designing and implementing an effective ICP does not need to be complicated or confusing, but does require thoughtful design and effective communication. It is important to understand that a sound ICP will not change behavior if it is used in

isolation; instead, it is intended to support changes in behavior to produce desired results.

The most essential ingredient for a successful ICP is good communication. Directly and personally communicating the intention and the mechanics of an ICP establishes trust in the concept and its execution. People must understand the goals and what they or their team must do to earn the incentive.

There will be times during the implementation and operation of an ICP when questions arise. If they are met with an open and constructive attitude, they can be instrumental in fostering a positive attitude that enhances the value of the program and its results. In addition, employees will become strong supporters of the company's efforts and direction.

Part IV

Conclusion

*"We are what we repeatedly do.
Therefore excellence is not an act
but, rather, a habit."*

Aristotle

Plan to Succeed
Success is no accident

Top-Down Vision and Bottom-Up Management can be an exciting and beneficial experience for all of its participants. For most companies, it will not be business as usual; significant changes in culture, relationships and management style are needed to make a successful transition to this collaborative environment.

Change starts at the top. The chief executive officer and other senior managers must commit to change. Their unhesitating dedication to Top-Down Vision and Bottom-Up Management prompts employees to respond with enthusiasm. However, even the most resolute commitment will be challenged by the stresses that all businesses experience regularly. At these times, employees will be looking for evidence to confirm their suspicions that this is just the latest "flavor of the month."

or most companies, it will not be usiness as usual. Significant changes in ulture, relationships and management yle are needed to make a successful ansition to this collaborative environment.

Difficult circumstances provide management an excellent opportunity to demonstrate its resolve. Even in the face of a crisis that presents the temptation to revert to command-and-control management, the commitment to Top-Down Vision and Bottom-Up Management must be maintained.

Top-Down Vision and Bottom-Up Management is built on the belief that most employees who are treated fairly, consistently and respectfully want to help their company succeed. The company's success is dependent on their support. Employees have th potential to be highly energized and creative. They need direction Tell them where the organiza tion would like to go. Explai why this approach is likel to lead to success. Involv them in the process of ge ting there. They will becom crusaders for the company cause, committed to turnin the Vision into reality.

> *To channel the abundant energy that becomes available, it is imperative to provide employees with a Vision that unambiguously points them in the direction of success.*

The power unleashed by To Down Vision and Bottom-Up Management creates enormou opportunities and obligations for leaders. To channel the abundar energy that becomes available, it is imperative to provide employ ees with a Vision that unambiguously points them in the directio of success. Whereas in the past managers might have felt tha it was their responsibility to be in the trenches with their team they must now spend significantly more time working on deve oping a Vision, ensuring appropriate buy-in, removing barriers employee success and functioning as coaches and cheerleader

Top-Down Vision and Bottom-Up Management provides system to guide an organization through the process of chang The complexities of most businesses dictate that this journe be conducted over a period of weeks or months. It may tempting to conclude that the pressures of day-to-day busine take precedence and leave no time for a time-consuming pla ning process. The consequences of succumbing to this thin ing are why a company needs to determine how to make tin for success. Very few businesses achieve sustained succe unless they invest energy and resources to create a downh ride that facilitates success without corporate exhaustion.

The team-based approach of Top-Down Vision and Bottom-L

Management involves people throughout a company, spreading the workload, promoting creative problem solving and unleashing inherent talents and capabilities. The resulting collaboration and motivation support personal fulfillment and business success. We can all dream about achieving success, but we can experience it only if we take appropriate action to increase the odds, whether in our personal or business lives. This book sets out a path to success for businesses, whether large or small, following a systematic and logical methodology.

The starting point is to understand the context, or environment and conditions in which the business and its markets are operating. The chief executive officer and the senior management team prepare a draft or "straw man" Vision for the business. They must take into account the context, projections of what the future market leader will look like and an evaluation of the company's past and likely future strategic biases. Teams and individuals throughout the company are then established to review and comment on the Vision. Next, they help in developing the strategies needed to execute the Vision. Those teams then take the lead role in identifying and implementing the specific tactics to achieve success.

> We can all dream about achieving success, but we can experience it only if we take appropriate action to increase the odds.

The result is a comprehensive plan that has buy-in— the key catalyst for successful implementation. Determined and committed leadership with a great plan and company-wide buy-in positions a business to proceed along the exciting and rewarding path to success. We have witnessed scores of businesses achieve dramatic and lasting improvements— resulting in great financial success and personal satisfaction. Similar outcomes are available to all businesses that embrace the principles of Top-Down Vision and Bottom-Up Management.

Checklist for
Current State Analysis

Porter's[1] Five Forces of Industry Structure Framework

- Supplier power
- Buyer power
- Threat of substitutes
- Threat of new entrants
- Rivalry
- Also need to assess impact from government/regulatory, technological and economic forces/factors

Market Size, Growth and Share

- Aggregate size
- Size by segment (customer and product)
- Distribution of relative market shares
- Expected market growth
- Expected growth by segment (customer and product)
- Level of regulation (especially on pricing)

Customer Dynamics

- Purchase process analysis
- Satisfaction levels
- Price elasticity analysis
- Product benefit analysis
- Promotional or marketing support required
- Customer market analysis (same as above, but for customers' markets)

---

1. Michael E. Porter, "How Competitive Forces Shape Strategy," *Harvard Business Review*, March-April, 1979.

Checklist for
Current State Analysis, *continued*

Financial Analysis

- Trends in operating performance metrics (Gross Profits EBITDA, key financial ratios benchmarked especiall ROE, ROAM, Debt to Equity)
- Performance versus peer group

Competitor Analysis

- Number and relative size
- Market share analysis
- Financial analysis
- Sales channel evaluation (estimate % of revenues by chan nel)
- Major customers served
- Competency analysis
- Vertical/horizontal integration/presence
- Perceived strategy (low cost, quality, value, etc)

Customer Analysis

- Evaluation of key performance criteria
- Evaluation of key drivers of purchase decision
- Analysis of suppliers used and level of satisfaction
- Sales distribution (percent of total sales represented b each customer, breadth of services or products purchase etc.)
- Switching costs

Checklist for
Current State Analysis, *continued*

Internal Company Analysis
- Financial analysis
- Five-year trends in sales and profits, EBITDA
- SWOT analysis
- Market share trends
- Customer satisfaction evaluation
- Process analysis
- Product line or portfolio analysis (contributions to sales, profits and requirements for working capital)
- Employee turnover

Setup Observation Form

Step	Description	Time	INT/EXT	E,G,PA,M*	Remarks and Observations

* Exchange, Gather, Position, Adjust, Muda (waste)

Appendix 3

Process Documentation Form

Process & Opportunity Notes

#	Description of Steps	VA	NVA	Time	Travel Dist.
1					
2					
3					
4					
5					
6					
7					
8					
9					
10					
11					
12					
13					
14					
15					
16					
17					
18					
19					
20					
Total					

Sample Daily Flash Report

Element	Day	MTD	Goal	+/- Goal
Open Orders This Month		293,262	607,041	-313,779
Open Orders Next Month		33,429	1,220,000	-1,186,571
Open Orders — 2 Months		138,129	1,277,000	-1,088,871
All Future Open Orders		283,845		
Total Open Orders		748,665		
Invoiced	8,787	23,959	162,839	-138,880
New Orders Received	81,439	228,791	1,220,000	-991,109
Backorders	492	83,258	0	83,258
DSO		44	42	-2.00
DPO		65	60	5.00
Inventory Turns		3.4	4.0	-0.60
Lines Shipped Complete	98.00%	98.00%	95%	3.00%
Shipments On Time & Complete	94%	86%	80%	6.00%
Dollars Shipped On Time	42%	79%	95%	-16.17%
Raw Material		4,987,356	5,050,000	-62,644
Finished Goods		1,358,404	1,540,000	-181,596
Total Inventory		6,345,760	6,590,000	-244,240
Actual Hours		2,950		
Earned Hours		1,848		
% Effective (A)		62.65%	70.00%	-7.35%
% Utilization (B)		85.38%	90.00%	-4.62%
Total Effectiveness - (A*B)		53.49%	63.00%	-9.51%
Direct/Indirect Employee Ratio	5.40	5.2	5.00	0.20
Sales Dollars Per Labor Hour Actual Hrs		8	10	-2
Sales Dollars Per Labor Hour TD Hrs		13	12	1
Sales Dollars Retail	7,898	38,605	227,300	-188,695
Sales Per Transaction	10	10	8.00	2
Sales Per Labor Hour		31	37.15	-6
Wage % of Sales Dollars		25.00%	22.90%	2.10%
Overtime		2.00%	1.00%	1.00%
% First Pass Yield	98.51%	97.80%	99.00%	-1.20%

Sample Hourly Tracking Chart

Time	Actual	Goal	+/- Goal
8AM	90	100	-10
9AM	200	200	0
10:15AM	310	300	+10
11:15AM	400	400	0
12:45AM	475	500	-25
1:45PM	590	600	-10
2:45PM	705	700	+5
4:00PM	800	800	0

Problems: Absent employee caused late start and training issues

First shift total — 800
Second shift total — 750
Third shift total — 825

Glossary

NOTE TO READER: *All words in full capitals refer to terms defined in the glossary.*

ABC – See ACTIVITY-BASED COSTING.

ACTIVITY-BASED COSTING – The actual cost of a product or service based on all the activities directly involved in the development, production and delivery of the product or service. Also known as ABC.

ADVISORY TEAM – Cross-functional and multi-level team that acts as a source of ideas and also as a sounding board for senior management.

ASSET TURNOVER RATES – Sales divided by total assets.

ATTRIBUTABLE COSTS – Expenditures that can be directly related to a product, product line or department.

BATCH FORMAT – Materials or paperwork moving through a business from department to department in batches or piles. Production in this format is characteristically based on economic order sizes (EOQ) independent of actual customer demand.

BOTTOM-UP MANAGEMENT – Leaders and employees at all levels are involved in making a company's VISION a reality.

BRAINSTORMING – Generating ideas in a group situation based on the principles of suspended judgment and cross-stimulation.

BUY-IN – Commitment of employees of a company to its VISION for the future.

CELLULAR PROCESSING – All activities in a process are arranged in close proximity, resembling a cell, and processing takes place in a CONTINUOUS FLOW. The typical cell is U-shaped and flows counterclockwise.

CHANGE LOOP – A process that helps to identify key initiatives, the difficulty in implementing them and the potential impact of their implementation.

CHANGEOVER – The process of changing the SETUP of a machine so that production can be switched to a different item.

COMPETITIVE ADVANTAGES – Advantages that allow a business to survive and thrive over the long haul. Examples: patents, reliability, speed of turnaround, lower costs, status, employees and service.

CONSENSUS BUILDING – Group decision-making process in which every participant's input is carefully considered and the best possible outcome to meet the needs of the group is crafted.

CONTEXT – The company and market evolution.

CONTINUOUS FLOW – Processing method that groups different functional areas of expertise required for a specific process into the same area, enabling products or paperwork to move more rapidly through the process. When an activity is completed, it is immediately passed on to the next activity rather than waiting for a pile to be completed and moved. Also known as one-piece flow or single-piece flow.

CYCLE TIME – Elapsed time from the first step in a process to the time the process is complete.

DEMOGRAPHIC ANALYSIS – Statistical analysis of characteristics of people (age, income, etc.) used to identify markets.

DRIVERS OF SUCCESS – Specific elements of business performance that a company will focus on and measure.

EBITDA – Earnings before interest, taxes, depreciation and amortization.

EXTERNAL ACTIVITIES – CHANGEOVER work that can be done while a machine is in operation.

FILL RATES – Percentage of total orders filled per invoice shipped. Measure can include dollars filled, line items filled or items filled (also known as "eaches" filled).

FISHBONE DIAGRAMS – An analytical tool that provides a methodical way of looking at effects and the causes that create or contribute to those effects. Useful for studying reasons for a problem.

FIXED COSTS – Costs that tend to remain unchanged when sales volumes fluctuate.

FLASH REPORT – Timely and accurate feedback on key measurables about how a company is performing relative to stated objectives. Provides employees with the essential information needed to assess and improve performance.

FULL-ABSORPTION ACCOUNTING – Allocates general types of overhead costs to the cost of products or services.

FUNCTIONAL TEAM – Team set up to perform specific regular function in a business. More permanent in nature than PROJECT TEAM. Could extend from team working together in a department (example: accounts receivable team) to cross-functional teams that focus on a process that crosses many boundaries (example: product development team).

GAAP – Acronym for generally accepted accounting principles. A common set of accounting principles, standards and procedures issued by standard-setting bodies whose purpose is to standardize financial accounting.

GAINSHARING PLAN – Reward system for all employees that is consistent with the long-term interests of a company. Known as ICP, or INCENTIVE COMPENSATION PLAN.

INCENTIVE COMPENSATION PLAN (ICP) – Reward system for employees that is consistent with the long-term interests of a company. Known as GAINSHARING PLAN.

INTERNAL ACTIVITIES – CHANGEOVER work that can be performed only when the machine is "down" (not in operation).

JIT (Just-in-time) – Producing just what is needed, when it is needed, in the amount needed with the minimum materials, equipment, labor and space.

KAIZEN – A technique for analyzing and improving processes. Empowers employees in a team format to help a company make improvements that enable it to move closer to its VISION.

KANBAN – Simple visual signals to initiate action or activity to facilitate a JIT mode.

LEAN – The speeding up of processes throughout business by eliminating waste and inefficiency.

MANDATE – Assignment given team that defines specific objective, timetable, boundaries and level of authority.

MICRO-NICHE – A more focused or specialized part of a market niche.

MIND MAPPING®[1] – Graphic problem-solving technique. A brainstorming alternative for improved learning and clearer thinking.

NON-ATTRIBUTABLE COSTS – Expenditures that are not directly related to the production of an item.

NON-VALUE-ADDED ACTIVITIES (NVAs) – Actions that consume time, resources or space, but do not add to the value of a product or service.

---

1.   Mind Mapping is a registered trademark of The Buzan Group, 1990.

PARETO PRINCIPLE – Only a few factors are responsible for most problems.

PROJECT TEAM – Team formed with a specific purpose or unique task, such as a team formed to improve productivity in a department.

NVA – See NON-VALUE-ADDED ACTIVITIES.

OVER-PRODUCTION – Producing more inventory than is needed to respond to customers' immediate needs.

POKA-YOKE – Error proofing.

PULL-THROUGH SCHEDULING – Production processes do not begin until the customer gives the signal, usually represented by a purchase order or a KANBAN signal.

RAAP – Accounting information acronym based on real-time, activity-based, accountability-focused performance data.

REAL-TIME INFORMATION – Vital information about an event as close to the event as possible.

RETURN ON INVESTMENT – Determines the percentage return on funds invested. Also known as ROI.

ROAM – Return on assets managed.

ROE – Return on equity.

ROI – See RETURN ON INVESTMENT.

SETUP – The process of setting up or preparing a machine so that it is able to produce the items needed.

SILOS – Departments are referred to as silos because information and span of authority are confined to a small part of the business, with little communication and cooperation between them.

SMED/Single-Minute Exchange of Dies – A systematic approach to reduce SETUP times from one product to another with the goal of reducing the time of setups to a single digit and even eventually eliminating setups.

SPAN OF CONTROL – Appropriate control over all of the key elements of the task for which a person or team is given responsibility.

STORYBOARDING – Technique used to organize and display information and brainstorm ideas.

STRATEGIES – Major actions, activities or capabilities that must be put in place to make the VISION a reality.

STRAW MAN – Proposed conceptual VISION statement.

SWOT – Acronym for strengths, weaknesses, opportunities, threats. Used as framework for future state analysis. Looks internally for a company's strengths and weaknesses. Also identifies external opportunities and threats that are most likely to affect a business in the foreseeable future.

TACTICS – Specific steps that must be taken to ensure that a desired strategy is implemented.

TAKT – A German word that means beat of the drum. In KAIZEN, it means the pace of customer demand.

TDVBUM – TOP-DOWN VISION AND BOTTOM-UP MANAGEMENT.

THROUGHPUT – The amount of product or services produced or delivered in a period of time in a given process.

TOP-DOWN VISION – Senior management develops a company's VISION and then communicates it to all employees and engages their commitment.

UTILIZATION RATES – Percentage of total capacity utilized.

VA – See VALUE-ADDED ACTIVITIES.

VALUE-ADDED ACTIVITIES – Actions that transform or shape raw material, information or services to meet internal or external customers' needs. Also known as VAs.

VALUE PROPOSITION – Defines what the company is offering to customers that creates enough value to warrant parting with their money in exchange.

VALUE STREAM – The symbolic river of VALUE-ADDED ACTIVITIES that are necessary to produce a product or deliver a service, from conception to customer. Activities that are not value-added are symbolic diversions of the river's most efficient flow, extending process times and contributing to poor quality.

VARIABLE COSTS – Expenditures that tend to occur in proportion to sales.

VISION – Inspiring and ambitious plan for the future of a business developed by senior management. Serves as the guide for all decision making.

WIN RATIO – Percentage of total deals, sales, etc. finalized relative to total opportunities presented.

5-S – An organized and systematic approach to housekeeping and workplace organization to improve efficiency and drive out waste.

Answer for the inspection challenge in the chapter titled Error Proofing in Part III: The letter f appears 44 times.

Index

Accountability
    information systems to support,
        175-176
    Vision filter, 63-64
    Vision, need for, 7
Accounting, real, Tool 3, 159-178
    activity-based costing, 165-174
    direct/indirect labor, 165-176
    fixed costs, 166-174
    flash reports, 23, 163-164, 175
    full-absorption accounting, 165-174
    GAAP, definition, 161
    product profit margin, 170-174
    RAAP, definition, 161
    real-time information, 163-164
    variable costs, 166-174
Action plan development, 100-103
Activity-based costing. See also
        Full-absorption costing
    definition, 165
    direct labor/indirect labor, 165-176
    real costs, 165-168
Advisory teams. See Employee advisory-
        teams and Teams
Apple Computer, 47

Barriers to success, 19, 71, 220
Batch processing
    defects, 133
    definition, 122
    problems of, 122-124
    setups and changeovers, 127-128
Bennis, Warren, 20
Bite-sized pieces, 80, 175-176
Bottom-Up Management
    brainstorming and analytical
        techniques, 179-207
    definition, 76

employees' responsibility for, 4
    gainsharing, 211-215
    Kaizen, 151-158
    people power, unleashing, 75-76
    senior management's commitment to,
        219-221
    tactics, 98-105
    teams. See Teams
Brainstorming and analytical techniques,
        Tool 4, 181-207
    change loop, 200-201
    consensus building, 193-195
    facilitator, 181-183, 205-207
    fishbone diagrams, 184-186
    ground rules, 181-183, 207
    identifying strategies, 87
    Mind Mapping®, 196-198
    Pareto analysis, 202-203
    productive meetings, 205-207
    storyboarding, 187-191
    tactics, 99-100
British Airways, 57
Buy-in
    brainstorming, generating, 181-183
    catalyst for success, 27-28
    essential ingredient, 27
    process, 26

Capital structure, 59
Change, 219-221
Change loop, 200-201
Changeovers. See also Batch processing
        and Setups
    continuous flow, 127-132
    SMED, 116
Collaboration
    advisory teams, 70
    continuous flow environment, 121

Collaboration, *continued*
  correlation with success, 3-4
  differing roles, 4
  importance of attitude, 20
  management style, changing, 3-5,
    17-20, 75-76, 219-221
  teams, power of, 77-82
  transition to, 219-221
  Vision, 50
Command-and-control management,
  death of, 3-5
Communication
  flash reports, 23, 163-164, 175
  leaders' energies, allocation of, 7
  poor performance, 19
  silos, 78-79
  successful incentive compensation
    plan, 215
  teams, benefits of, 77
Competitive advantage/edge
  dominating niches, 13
  employees, 25, 58, 75-76
  outperforming the competition, 13
  reasons to thrive, 57-58
Consensus building, 193-195
Context
  current state analysis, 35-41
  definition of, 31
  future market leader, 48-49
  future state analysis, 35, 41-42
  industry evolution analysis, 41-43
  market structure analysis, 39-41
  SWOT analysis, 36-39
Continuous flow. *See also* Batch
    processing
  building block of Lean, 114-116
  changeovers, 127-132
  customer demand, meeting, 121-126
  takt time, 155-157
Continuous improvement
  Vision filter, 65
Costs
  attributable and non-attributable,
    171-174
  fixed and variable, 166-174
  incentive compensation plans, 213

Creativity
  brainstorming, 181
  employees, 76
  enhanced by teams, 77-82
  implementing Lean, 117
  Kaizen events, 153-154
Current state analysis, *See* Context
Customers
  balancing demand and production,
    145-147
  response time, 121-126, 149
  revering, 62
  targeting, 56-57
Cycle times
  Kaizen teams, 155-158
  reducing, 115, 149-150

Defects. *See also* Inventory
  error proofing, 133-135
Dell Computer Corporation, 126
Direct labor/indirect labor, 165-176
Downhill rides, 11-13, 64-65, 220
Drivers of success
  definition, 93
  elements of Vision statement, 94
  identifying, importance of, 94-95
  sharing with employees, 23

Employee advisory teams. *See also*
    Teams
  definition, 70
  members, selection of, 84
  types of teams, 83-85
  Vision verification, 70
Employees. *See also* Brainstorming and
    Collaboration
  accountability, 175-176
  "Aha!" test, 15-16
  buy-in, 26, 27-28, 181-183
  collaboration with management, 3-5,
    17-20, 219-221
  competitive advantage, 25, 58, 75-76
  creativity, 76
  motivating, 15-16
  people power, 75

roadblocks to success, 8, 19
sensitive information, sharing, 21-24
support from management, 7-8
teams, 77-82
teamwork, 121
trust, 27-28, 76
unleashing, 75-76
VIPs, 25
Enron, 54
Error proofing, 133-135, 157-158
External activities. *See also* Setups
   definition, 128-129

Facilitator
   brainstorming, 181-183
   techniques and skills, 205-207
Filters, Vision, 61-65
Fishbone diagrams, 184-186
Fixed costs, 166-174
Flash reports, 23, 163-164, 175
Focus
   outsourcing, 65
   Vision filter, 61-62
Full-absorption accounting
   compared to activity-based
      accounting, 165-168
Future market leader, 48-49
Future state analysis. *See* Context

GAAP. *See* Accounting
Gainsharing
   incentive compensation plan, 213-215
   supporting focus on Vision, 211
Gap analysis
   developing strategies, 87-88
   future market leader, 48-49
GE, 116 n4
Gretzky, Wayne, 36
Growth rate, 58

Home Depot, 59

Industry evolution analysis, 41-43

Information
   flash reports, 23, 163-164, 175
   performance data, 177-178
   real-time, 163-164
Internal activities. *See also* Setups
   definition, 128
   reducing setup and changeover time,
      127-133
Inventory. *See also* Setups
   batch manufacturing, 124
   benefits of reducing, 149-150
   error proofing to reduce, 133-135
   Lean operations, 124-126
   process cycle time, reducing, 125-126
   takt time, using to regulate, 144-147

JIT. *See* Just-in-time
Just-in-time
   building block of Lean, 114

Kaizen event/process, 141, 151-158
Kanban, 114
Kelleher, Herb, 9
Kennedy, President John F., 10
King, Rollin, 9

Leaders, 17-20. *See also* Managers,
   senior
   allocation of energies, 6-8
   authority, using sparingly, 17
   barriers to success, removing, 8, 19
   definition of true leaders, 17
   managers functioning as, 17
   motivating employees, 17-20
   teams, 80
   VIPs, 25
   Vision, responsibility for, 10, 67-68
Lean, Tool 1, 111-150
   activity-based costing, 165-168, 170-
      174
   batch processing versus continuous
      flow, 121-126
   benefits, 113, 149-150
   buckets of waste, 118
   building blocks of Lean systems, 114-117

Lean, Tool 1, *continued*
cornerstone of TDVBUM, 114
customer demand, 121-126
definition, 113
error proofing, 133-135
reducing setup and changeover time,
127-132
takt time as cornerstone, 144-147
value stream, mapping, 119, 137-142

Managers, senior. *See also* Leaders
accountability, 175-176
alliance with employees, 4
allocation of energies, 6-8
coaching employees, 8, 20
collaboration, transition to, 17-20,
75-76, 219-221
command-and-control style, 3-5
context analysis, 35-43
input from employees, 8
job number one, 7-8
management style, 219-221
role model, 20
sharing sensitive information, 21-24
VIPs, 25
Vision, responsibility for, 7-8, 10,
67-68
Vision, verifying, 69-71
Mandates, 80, 158
Marcus, Bernie, 59
Market structure analysis, 39-41
Micro-niche, 13
Mind Mapping®, 196-198
Mission statement
differentiated from Vision statement,
15
Motivation
collaborative partnership, 3-5
gainsharing, 211-215
unleashing employees, 17-20, 75-76
Vision statement as catalyst, 15-16

Niche, 12-13
Non-value-added activities. *See also*
Value-added activities

definition, 119
examples, 118, 156
Kaizen teams to identify and
eliminate, 155-158
Lean environment, 119-120
operating costs, 149
setups and changeovers, 128-132
value stream mapping, 137-142

Opportunities. *See* SWOT analysis,
36-39
Outsourcing, 61-62, 65

Pareto analysis, 202-203
Partnership. *See* Collaboration
People power
unleashing, 61, 75-76
Performance data, 177. *See also* Flash
reports
Porter's Five Forces, 40-41
Priorities, balancing, 104
Productivity. *See also* Continuous flow
Bottom-Up Management Tool 1,
111-150
Lean as catalyst for, 113-116,
119-120, 126
relentless pursuit of, 120
Profitability, 59
Process improvement
facilitated by teams, 79
restricted by silos, 78-79

RAAP, 161
Relationships, 4
Roadblocks to success
employees, evaluating, 19
removing, 8

Sensitive information, 21-24
concerns about sharing, 21
drivers of success, 23
importance of sharing, 21
using graphs, 23

Setups. *See also* Batch processing and
    Continuous flow
  internal and external activities,
    definition of, 128-129
  reducing, 127-132
  videotaping changeover, 130-131
Shingo, Shigeo, 133
Silos, 78-79
Southwest Airlines, 9-10, 13, 54, 57
Span of control, 78
Storyboarding, 187-191
Strategies
  activity-based costing to determine, 91
  brainstorming, 87
  components, 96-97
  80:20 Rule, 88
  gap analysis, 87-88
  identifying and developing, 87-92
  prioritizing, 88
Straw man, 50
Strengths. *See* SWOT analysis, 36-39
Success
  buy-in, 27-28
  correlation with collaboration, 3-4
  downhill rides, 11-13, 64-65, 220
  driven by Vision, 7-8
  planning for, 219-221
  secrets of, 24
  VIPs, 25
  Vision statement, 16
  Vision statement filters, 61-65
  SWOT analysis, 36-39

Tactics
  action plan development, 100-103
  brainstorming, 99-100
  components, 106-107
  execution of strategies, 98-105
Takt time, 144-147, 155-157
Teams. *See also* Employee advisory teams
  accountability, 175-176
  action plan development, 100-103
  advisory, 83-85
  brainstorming, 181-183
  consensus building, 193-195
  functional, 83

ground rules, 81
Kaizen, Tool 2, 153-158
Lean, implementing, 117
levels of authority, 80
mandates, 80, 158
members, selection, 84
power of, 77-82
productive meetings, 205-207
project, 83,85
tactics, brainstorming, 99-103
timely information, need for, 161,
    163-164
types, 83-85
value of, 85
Threats. *See* SWOT analysis, 36-39
Titanic, 69
Top-Down Vision and Bottom-Up
    Management
  appropriateness for all companies, 5
  benefit of implementing, 5
  Lean as cornerstone, 114
  stages of, 31-32
Top-Down Vision, stages of, 31-32
Trust, 27-28, 76, 158

Value-added activities. *See also* Non-
    value-added activities
  definition, 119
  Kaizen teams to identify, 155-158
  setups and changeovers, 127-132
  value stream mapping 137-142
Value proposition, 57
Value stream, 116, 119, 137-142, 145
Variable costs, 166-174
Videotaping, 130-131
VIPs, 25
Vision
  accountability, 175-176
  bias, 46-48
  buy-in, 27-28
  context for, 35-43
  definition, 31
  differentiating from strategies and
    tactics, 104-105
  drivers of success, 93-95
  filters, 61-65

Vision, *continued*
  guiding light, 5, 7,10, 45-46
  implementing with teams, 80
  job number one, 7-8
  management's responsibility for, 4,7,
    67-68
  objective, 15-16
  painting a picture of the future, 9-10
  periodic review of, 50
  proactive leadership, 11
  straw man, 50
  summary, 53
  SWOT analysis, 36-39
  values, core corporate, 45
  verification, need for, 69-71
Vision Statement
  "Aha!" test, 15-16
  components, 52-59
  customers/markets, 56-58
  definition, 16
  filters, 61-65
  finance, 58-59
  mission statement, differentiated from,
    15
  objective, 15
  operations, 54-56
  people/culture, 53-54
  value proposition, 57

Wal-Mart, 46-47, 57
Waste
  buckets of, 118
  using takt time to eliminate, 145
  value stream, identifying, 116-120
Weaknesses. *See* SWOT analysis, 36-39
Welch, Jack, 7